거의 모든 **일상**
표현 의 영어

케빈 강 (강진호)

美 Illinois State Univ. 언어치료학 최우등 졸업
美 Univ. of Memphis 이중언어 박사 과정 1년 수료
美 멤피스 언어청각센터 언어치료사 (Graduate Clinician)
前 강남 이익훈 어학원 영어발음 / 스피킹 대표 강사
前 스피킹핏 영어센터 대표 강사
現 링고애니 대표

저서 〈특허받은 영어발음 & 리스닝〉, 〈영어단어 그림사전〉,
〈미국 영어와 영국 영어를 비교합니다〉, 〈영어 발음은 이런 것이다〉
〈영어 단어의 결정적 뉘앙스들〉, 〈영어 발음 향상 훈련〉, 〈영어 표현의 결정적 뉘앙스들〉

해나 변 (변혜윤)

美 Judah Christian School / Oldfields School 졸업
日 Ritsumeikan Univ. 국제관계학 졸업
캐나다 Global College TESOL 및 GETQA 국제 영어 교사 자격증
前 국제 심포지엄 외국인 전담 동시통역사
前 UNICEF 한국위원회 팀원
現 Hanna's English 대표

거의 모든 일상 표현의 영어

지은이 케빈 강, 해나 변
초판 1쇄 발행 2022년 11월 1일
초판 11쇄 발행 2024년 10월 7일

발행인 박효상 **편집장** 김현 **기획 · 편집** 장경희, 이한경 **디자인** 임정현
마케팅 이태호, 이전희 **관리** 김태옥

기획 · 편집 진행 김현 **본문 · 표지디자인** 고희선

녹음 제작 믹스캠프 스튜디오 **콘텐츠 제작 지원** 석근혜, 유수빈, 이종학(케쌤)
종이 월드페이퍼 **인쇄 · 제본** 예림인쇄 · 바인딩

출판등록 제10-1835호 **발행처** 사람in **주소** 04034 서울시 마포구 양화로 11길 14-10 (서교동) 3F
전화 02) 338-3555(代) **팩스** 02) 338-3545 **E-mail** saramin@netsgo.com
Website www.saramin.com

ISBN
978-89-6049-975-1 14740
978-89-6049-936-2 세트

우아한 지적만보, 기민한 실사구시 사람in

거의 모든 일상 표현의 영어

아침
기상에서
밤에
잠들기까지

소소한
일상을
영어로
표현합니다!

스팀 다리미로 옷을 관리하다
take care of
one's clothes with
a
standing
STEAM
IRON

해외 고객들과
화상회의를 하다

HOLD
a videoconference
with overseas clients

(평소보다/일부러) 늦잠 자다
sleep IN

넥타이를 고쳐 매다
FIX
ONE'S TIE

변동 금리로
주택 담보 대출을 받다
take out a
VARIABLE
-RATE
mortgage (loan)

LIE DOWN and USE THE INTERNET ON ONE'S SMARTPHONE

텐트를 치고 캠핑하다

Pitch
A TENT
and
CAMP

에어프라이어로
요리하다
cook
in
an
air
fryer

시식 코너에서
제품 맛을 보다
Try
a FREE-
SAMPLE
at
the booth

누워서
스마트폰으로
인터넷을 하다

DAILY EXPRESSIONS

케빈 강, 해나 변 지음

사람in

'나의 일상을 영어로 표현한다면?'
이 질문에 던지는 깔끔한 대답

평범한 일반 사람들은 아침에 일어나서 나갈 준비를 하고 학교나 일터로 향합니다. 저녁이면 돌아와 하루를 마무리하고 내일을 맞을 준비를 하고 잠자리에 들지요. 주말이나 휴가 때는 여행을 가기도 하고, 각자의 종교에 따라 종교 생활을 하기도 합니다.

이런 일련의 과정에서 보이는 우리의 모습은 회화와 작문의 중요한 소재입니다. 지인들과의 대화를 분석해 보면 더 확실합니다. 원어민과의 대화라고 다를까요? 주말을 보내고 만난 외국인 친구와 이야기할 때 주말에 했던 일, 주말에 있었던 일이 주제가 됩니다. 그때 자신의 일상을 영어로 말하면서 본격적인 대화는 시작되고, 그걸 통해 상대방을 알아가고 인간관계가 쌓입니다. 더 심도 깊은 의사소통의 소중한 단초가 되는 일상 표현을 절대 소홀히 해서는 안 되고, 일상과 관련된 표현을 따로 익혀야 하는 중요한 이유이지요.

이런 중요성을 알기에 '보통 사람의 하루 + 주말/휴가 일상'을 통해 우리가 평소에 어떤 모습을 하는지, 어떤 상태에 놓이는지, 그리고 그것을 영어로 어떻게 표현하는지를 이 〈거의 모든 일상 표현의 영어〉에 담았습니다.

이런 일상 표현을 다른 어떤 것보다 먼저 공부해야 하는 이유는, 익숙한 것을 영어로 알아가는 즐거움이 있기 때문입니다. 무엇이든 꾸준히 하려면 재미가 있고 즐거워야 합니다. 한 번도 쓸 일 없는 어렵고 현학적인 표현 대신 자신에게 친숙한 것을 영어로 알게 되면서 어렵게만 보이던 영어가 조금은 만만하게 느껴지고, 바로 이때가 영어 학습의 지속성을 좌우하는 포인트가 되는 것입니다.

아침에 눈을 떠서 알람 시계를 무심코 누르는 동작이 영어로 무엇인지, 시리얼을 그릇에 담고 우유를 붓는 것이 영어로 무엇인지, 지하철 개찰구를 빠져나오는 것이 영어로 무엇인지 전에는 몰랐던 것들이 들어오고 말해 보고 싶어진다면, 그래서 그런 즐거움을 계속 느끼고 싶다면 책을 끝까지 보아 주세요. 그러다 보면 자기도 모르는 사이 굉장히 많은 표현을 알게 될 거고, 유창한 영어 회화자로 가는 길의 기초가 탄탄히 잡힌 것입니다.

이 책은 아침에 기상해서 하루 일과를 마치고 잠자리에 드는 그 사이 사이에 보통 사람들이 하는 일상의 행동과 상태를 영어로 표현했습니다. 물론 이것과 다른 일상을 사는 분들도 계시겠지만, 일반적인 사람들의 일상을 뽑았다 이해하시고 책을 봐 주시기 바랍니다.

처음부터 봐야 뒤의 내용을 이해할 수 있는 책이 아니라서 이 책은 아무 페이지부터 펼쳐서 시작해도 좋습니다. 목차를 보다가 관심 있는 부분을 찾아가서 시작해도 괜찮습니다. 중요한 건 포기하지 않고 끝까지 가는 것이니까요. '일주일 만에 다 끝내겠다, 한 달 안에 세 번을 읽겠다' 이런 다짐보다는 하루에 한 페이지라도 꾸준히, 공부하지 않고 지나가는 날이 없도록 하는 게 최고입니다. 낙숫물이 바위를 뚫듯이 꾸준히 하다 보면 잘 안 외워지던 것도 외워지고, 다른 영어 예문을 보다가 비슷한 내용을 만나면 확실히 자기 것이 되는 경험을 하게 될 것입니다.

각 유닛별 학습에서 추천하고 싶은 것은 한글 표현을 읽고 영어로는 어떻게 말할지 생각해 본 다음에 책에 나와 있는 영어 표현을 확인해 보는 것입니다. 처음에는 눈으로만, 두 번째 볼 때는 입으로 소리 내어, 세 번째 볼 때는 QR코드를 찍고 섀도잉하면서 한다면 효과가 있을 겁니다. 학습이 어느 정도 이루어졌다는 생각이 들면 인덱스에 있는 한글 표현을 보면서 영어로 말해 보고, 영어 표현을 보면서 우리말 뜻을 말해 보는 훈련을 해 보세요. 표현을 온전히 자기 것으로 만드는 과정이 될 것입니다.

영어 회화와 작문 실력 향상에 꼭 필요한《거의 모든 일상 표현의 영어》는
다음과 같이 구성되어 있습니다.

본문의 영어 표현과 SENTENCES TO USE의 영어 문장
을 원어민이 정확한 발음으로 녹음했습니다.

change [replace] a light-bulb는 change a light-bulb, replace a light-bulb로 [ ]는 다른 단어를 대입
해도 의미가 변하지 않는 걸 의미합니다. 이때, [ ] 안의
영어가 들어가는 표현을 다 녹음했습니다.

표현에서 water the plants / flowers / vegetables처
럼 /는 water the plants, water the flowers, water
the vegetables처럼 같은 위치의 단어를 해당 단어로
대체하면 다른 의미의 표현이 된다는 뜻입니다.

SENTENCES TO USE는 위에서 배운 표현이 실제 회화
나 작문에서 쓰이는 예를 보여줍니다.

앞에서 배운 내용이 실제로는 어떻게 회화
에서 응용되는지 회화 예문으로 확인합니다.
현장감 120%, 생생한 느낌의 회화는 확인
학습의 즐거움을 배가합니다.

어느 정도 학습이 되었다고 판단되면 인덱스의 한글 부분을
보면서 영어 표현을, 영어 부분을 보면서 우리말 표현을 말
해 보세요. 이렇게 하면 여러분의 어휘 실력이 몰라볼 만큼
성장할 것입니다.

차례

CHAPTER 1 기상 후 AFTER GETTING UP

CHAPTER 2 집안 일 HOUSEWORK

CHAPTER 3 이동 TRANSPORTATION

CHAPTER 4 장소 PLACES

CHAPTER 5   학교생활 SCHOOL LIFE

CHAPTER 6   직장 생활 LIFE AT WORK

CHAPTER 7   병원 HOSPITAL

CHAPTER 8   은행 BANK

CHAPTER

1

기상 후

AFTER GETTING UP

기상

알람 시계가 울리다
the alarm clock goes off [rings]

잠결에 몸을 뒤척이다
turn [roll] over in bed

스누즈 버튼
(몇 분 뒤 알람이 다시 울리는 타이머 버튼)을 누르다
hit the snooze button

알람 시계를 끄다
turn off the alarm clock

라디오를 켜다
turn on the radio

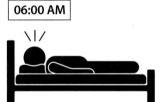

아침 6시에 잠이 깨다
wake up at 6 a.m.

SENTENCES TO USE

그는 아침 일찍 알람이 울리자 잠결에 몸을 뒤척였어요.
He turned over in bed as the alarm went off in the early morning.

저는 직장 때문에 보통 아침 7시에 일어나지만 주말에는 평소보다 늦잠을 잡니다.
I usually wake up at 7 a.m. for work, but I sleep in on the weekends.

비몽사몽 하다, 잠이 덜 깨다
be half asleep

아침에 일찍 일어나다
get up in the early morning

SAT 11:00 AM

주말에 늦게 일어나다
get up late on (the) weekends

from 9 PM to 6 AM

밤을 새우다
stay up all night, pull an all-nighter

(뜻하지 않게) 늦잠 자다
oversleep

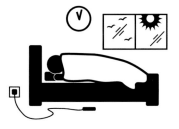

(평소보다/일부러) 늦잠 자다
sleep in

그녀는 수업 내내 비몽사몽 했어요.
She was half asleep throughout the whole class.

오늘 볼 퀴즈 준비하느라 나 밤 새웠어.
I pulled an all-nighter preparing for the quiz today.

나 오늘 늦잠 자서 학교 지각이네.
I overslept today and I am late for school.

침대에(잠자리에서 일어나) 앉아 기지개를 켜다
sit up in bed and stretch

안경을 쓰다
put one's glasses on

침대 밖으로 나오다
get out of bed

침대를 정돈하다
make one's bed

이부자리를 개다
fold up the bedding

불을 켜다
turn on the light

창문을 열다
open the window

바깥을 보다
look outside

SENTENCES TO USE

침대에 일어나 앉아 기지개를 켜는 게 하루를 시작하는 좋은 방법입니다.
Sitting up in bed and stretching is a good way to start the day.

저는 방을 나가기 전에 늘 침대를 정리합니다.
I always make my bed before I leave my room.

겨울에는 아침에 창문을 열지 않아요.
We don't open the windows in mornings during the winter.

이메일을 확인하다
check one's email

스마트폰 문자 메시지를 확인하다
check text messages on one's mobile phone

샤워 가운을 입다
put on a shower robe

운동복을 입다
put on one's sportswear [jogging suit]

방 밖으로 나오다
get out of [leave]
one's room

뉴스를 틀다/확인하다
turn on / check the news

저는 아침에 업무 이메일을 확인하는 습관이 있습니다.
I have a habit of checking my business email in the morning.

샤워 가운 좀 입어요. 바닥에 물 다 흘리고 있잖아요.
Please put on a shower robe. You are dripping all over the floor.

A 자기야, 일어나! 벌써 7시 30분이야.
▶ Honey, wake up! It's already 7:30 a.m.

B 아우, 조금만 더 자면 좋겠다.
● Argh… I wish I could sleep in a little.

A 그러다 늦어. 잘 잤어?
▶ You are going to be late. Did you sleep well?

B 아니, 잘 못 잤어. 온몸이 뻐근하네. 어젯밤 꿈자리도 뒤숭숭하고. 자기는 어때?
● No, I had a bad night. My whole body feels stiff. And I had a disturbing dream last night. How about you?

A 난 아주 잘 잤어. 늦었으니까 자기가 가서 먼저 씻어.
▶ I slept very well. You are late, so go freshen up first.

난 바로 아침 식사 준비할게.
▶ I am going to make breakfast right away.

B 알았어. 서두르면 늦지는 않을 거야.
● Alright, I won't be late if I hurry.

아침 인사

좋은 아침(이에요)!
Morning!
Good morning!

오늘 아침은 어떠세요?
How are you this morning?
How is your morning so far?

안녕하세요.
Good day to you.

"잘 잤어요"의 다양한 표현들

I slept well [soundly].
I had a good night (sleep).
I had a good night's sleep.
I had a fine night.
I got enough sleep.

2 아침 운동

MP3 004

조깅하다
go jogging

운동하다
do a workout,
work out

반려동물을 산책시키다
take one's pet for
a walk

산책로를 걷다
walk the trails

공원을 거닐다
take a walk
in the park

헬스장에 가다
go to the gym [fitness
center], hit the gym (비격식)

수영하다
go
swimming

산에 오르다(등산하다)
go
(mountain) hiking

* stretch는 명사,
  동사로 둘 다 쓰임.

스트레칭(을 하다)
stretch

요가를 하다
do yoga

줄넘기를 하다
skip [jump] rope

자전거를 타다
ride a bicycle

SENTENCES TO USE

제이크는 매일 아침 자기 개를 산책시킵니다.　　Jake takes his dog for a walk every morning.

퇴근 후에 헬스장에 가서 운동할래?
Do you want to go to the gym and work out after work?

저는 주말마다 등산하러 갑니다.　　I go hiking on the weekends.

저는 스트레칭과 요가로 하루를 시작합니다.　　I start the day with a stretch and yoga.

제 남동생은 매일 저녁 운동하려고 줄넘기를 하곤 했습니다.
My brother used to jump rope every evening to exercise.

A 아우~ 잠이 덜 깬 것 같이
비몽사몽 하네. 스트레칭 좀
해야지.
▶ Argh… It feels like I am still
half asleep. I need to stretch a
little.

B 미아 씨, 좋은 아침이에요.
오늘도 일찍 운동하러 나오셨네요.
● How are you this morning,
Mia? You are out early to
exercise again.

A 안녕하세요, 스미스 씨. 매일 아침
반려견 데리고 조깅하시다니
대단하십니다.
▶ Good morning, Mr. Smith.
It's amazing that you jog with
your dog every morning.

B 말도 마세요. 저희 개가
새벽 5시 반만 되면 산책 나가자고
깨워 대니 안 나올 수가 없어요.
● Tell me about it! I can't help
but come out when my dog
wakes me up every 5:30 a.m.
to go out for a walk.

A 이 녀석, 아주 부지런하네요!
그래서 그런지 개가 스미스 씨처럼
아주 건강해 보이는데요.
▶ This guy is very diligent!
Maybe that's why your dog
looks as healthy as you, Mr.
Smith.

B 네, 주변에 보면 아파서 병원에
자주 다니는 개들이 많은데
얘는 건강해서 다행이죠.
● True. I see a lot of dogs
around me that visit the vet
often due to illness, but I'm
glad my dog is healthy.

A 이 친구 나이가 어떻게 되나요?
▶ How old is your dog?

B 8살이요. 사람 나이로 치면
한 60살쯤 되려나요?
제 나이랑 비슷해요.
● He is 8 years old. About 60
in human age. Similar to my
age.

A 튼튼해 보여서 한 2~3살쯤 되겠다 했는데 생각보다 나이가 많군요.
▶ I thought he would be around 2~3 because he looks strong, but he is older than I thought.

스미스 씨처럼 젊어 보이는 거였네요. 하하.
▶ He looks as youthful as Mr. Smith. Haha.

B 아이고 별말씀을. 그럼, 좋은 하루 보내시고 다음에 또 봅시다.
● Oh my, what a compliment! Have a good day and see you next time.

A 선생님도 좋은 하루 보내세요.
▶ Have a nice day, too.

화장실에서 볼일을 보다
go to the bathroom

비데를 사용하다
use a bidet

변기 물을 내리다
flush the toilet

잠옷을 벗다
take off one's sleepwear

슬리퍼를 신다
put on slippers

손을 씻다
wash one's hands

세수하다
wash one's face

SENTENCES TO USE

비데 사용은 제 아침 일상에서 아주 중요한 부분입니다.
Using a bidet is a vital part of my morning routine.

아침 식사 전에 손 씻는 것 잊지 마세요.
Don't forget to wash your hands before breakfast.

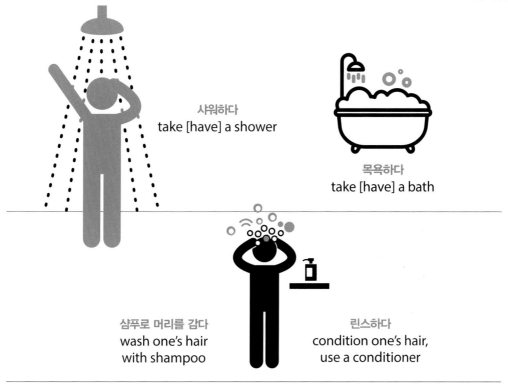

샤워하다
take [have] a shower

목욕하다
take [have] a bath

샴푸로 머리를 감다
wash one's hair
with shampoo

린스하다
condition one's hair,
use a conditioner

면도하다
shave

양치질하다
brush one's teeth

새라는 샴푸로 머리 감은 후 린스를 하지 않습니다.
Sarah does not use a conditioner after she washes her hair with shampoo.

그는 출근하기 전에 면도한다는 걸 잊었어요.
He forgot to shave before he left for work.

저는 보통 샤워하면서 양치질합니다.
I usually brush my teeth while I take a shower.

입을 (물로) 헹구다
rinse out one's mouth

가글하다
gargle

코를 풀다
blow one's nose

코를 파다
pick one's nose

면봉으로 귀를 파다
pick one's ears
with a cotton swab

얼굴에 스킨/로션/크림을 바르다
apply [put on] some toner /
lotion / cream on one's face

SENTENCES TO USE

저는 샤워 후에 면봉으로 귀를 팝니다.
I pick my ears with a cotton swab after taking a shower.

저는 항상 면봉으로 아이크림을 바릅니다.
I always apply eye cream with a cotton swab.

머리를 말리다
dry one's hair

머리를 빗다
comb one's hair

머리를 손질하다
do one's hair

화장을 하다
put on one's makeup,
put one's makeup on

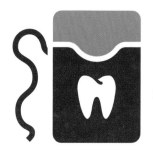

치실질을 하다
floss, use a floss

제 (여자) 조카는 매일 아침 머리 빗는 것을 싫어합니다.
My niece hates combing her hair every morning.

한나는 중요한 약속에 가기 전에 머리를 손질했습니다.
Hannah did her hair before she went off to an important appointment.

머리를 말리고 나서 화장을 해야 합니다.
I need to put my makeup on after drying my hair.

치과의사들은 양치질 후 치실질을 하라고 권합니다.
Dentists recommend using a floss after brushing teeth.

UNIT 4 아침 식사

아침 식사를 준비하다
prepare breakfast

아침 식사를 거르다
skip breakfast

아침 식사를 하다
eat [have] breakfast

정수기에서 물을 따르다
pour water from
the water purifier

과일 껍질을 벗기다
peel [skin] the fruit

* oil이
'기름을 두르다'의
동사로 쓰임.

프라이팬에 식용유를 두르다
oil the frying pan

프라이팬에 계란을 깨서 넣다
crack an egg into the pan

토스트를 만들다
make toast

빵에 잼을 바르다
spread some jam on bread

SENTENCES TO USE

엄마가 아침을 준비하는 동안 아빠는 커피를 내리세요.
My father makes coffee while my mother prepares breakfast.

엄마는 제가 절대 아침을 거르지 못하게 합니다.　　My mother never lets me skip breakfast.

항상 계란을 깨기 전에 팬에 기름 두르는 것을 기억하세요.
Always remember to oil the pan before cracking an egg into it.

토스트를 만드는 것이 제게는 가장 간단한 식사입니다.
Making toast is the simplest meal for me.

저는 빵에 블루베리 잼 대신 딸기 잼 바르는 걸 좋아해요.
I like to spread strawberry jam instead of blueberry jam on my bread.

냉장고에서 반찬들을 꺼내다
get some side dishes
out of the refrigerator

밥을 짓고 국을 끓이다
cook rice and soup

커피를 내리다
brew [make] coffee

시리얼을 그릇에 담다
pour cereal into
the bowl

시리얼 그릇에 우유를 붓다
pour milk into the
cereal bowl

전자레인지에 밥을 데우다
heat up the rice
in the microwave

상을 차리다
set the table

~와 음식을 나눠 먹다
share food with ~

도시락을 싸다
pack one's lunch [brown bag],
prepare one's lunch box

SENTENCES TO USE

식탁에 반찬 좀 꺼내 놔 주세요.
Please get some side dishes out on the table.

저는 우유를 붓기 전에 시리얼을 그릇에 담아요.
I pour cereal into the bowl before pouring milk.

저는 아침에 전자레인지에 밥 데우는 게 지겨워요.
I am sick of heating up rice in the microwave in the morning.

아침 먹게 상 좀 차려 주시겠어요?
Could you set the table for breakfast?

너 오늘은 도시락 싸지 않아도 돼.
You don't have to pack your lunch today.

A 아들, 엄마가 이따가 치울 테니까 밥 먹은 그릇 싱크대에 넣어 놔.
▶ Son, I will clean up later, so put your bowl in the sink.

B 네, 엄마. 나 이제 씻을게요.
● Okay, mom. I am going to wash up now.

A 늦었으니까 빨리 옷 갈아입고 양말 신고 양치해.
▶ You're late. Hurry up and change, put on your socks and brush your teeth.

B 앗, 책가방 챙기는 거 깜빡했어요.
● Oh, I forgot to pack my backpack.

A 자기 전에 다 챙겨 놨어야지.
▶ You should have packed it before you went to bed.

숙제는 다 했어?
▶ How about your homework?

B 네, 엄마. 숙제는 어제 다 끝냈죠.
● Yeah, mom. I finished it yesterday.

A 알았어. 도시락 잊어버리지 말고 잘 챙겨.
▶ Good. Don't forget your lunch box.

B 네, 엄마. 다녀오겠습니다.
● Okay. See you later, mom.

A 응, 선생님 말씀 잘 듣고, 친구랑 싸우지 말고 학교에서 즐겁게 있다 와.
▶ Yes, listen to your teachers, don't get into trouble with your friends, and have fun at school.

달걀 요리를 영어로

Hotel chef **How would you like your eggs?**
계란은 어떻게 해드릴까요?

Me '뭐라고 하지? 난 계란 프라이밖에 모르는데.'

해외 호텔이나 레스토랑에서 위의 문장을 들었을 때 난감했던 적이 있나요? 달걀은 요리 방법에 따라 다양하게 표현합니다. 지금부터 하나씩 배워 보세요.

raw egg: 날달걀

egg white(s): 달걀흰자

egg yolk: 달걀노른자

soft boiled: 삶은 달걀(반숙)

hard boiled: 삶은 달걀(완숙)

poached
: 수란(뜨거운 물에 달걀을 넣어 익힌 것)

omelet
: 오믈렛(달걀을 풀어 치즈, 고기, 채소 등을 넣어 부친 것)

scrambled
: 스크램블(달걀을 휘저어 만든 요리)

fried eggs: 계란 프라이

주의 '오므라이스'(omurice)는 일본어식 표기에서 유래된 음식으로 정확한 영어 표기는 그냥 omelet.

계란 프라이의 종류 (아래로 갈수록 완숙)

sunny-side-up
: 한 면만 익히고 노른자가 봉긋 올라온 프라이

over easy
: 양면 흰자만 살짝 익힌 프라이

over hard
: 양면 노른자까지 전부 익힌 프라이

Example

Q: How would you like your eggs?
계란은 어떻게 해드릴까요?

A: I would like my eggs **over easy**, please.
양쪽으로 흰자만 살짝 익힌 계란 프라이로 해 주세요.

Can I get a ham and cheese **omelet**?
햄 치즈 오믈렛 하나 주실래요?

I'll get two **hard boiled eggs** with the bacon.
베이컨과 함께 완숙으로 삶은 달걀 두 개 주세요.

I'd like mine **scrambled**, please.
저는 스크램블로 주세요.

Poached egg on the side would be great!
수란을 곁들여 주시면 좋을 것 같아요!

* put on은
옷을 입는 동작,
wear는 옷을
입고 있는 상태.

~을 입다
put on [wear] ~,
get dressed

속옷을 입다
put on [wear]
underwear

셔츠를 입다
put on [wear]
a shirt

스타킹을 신다
put on [wear]
one's stockings

바지를 입다
put on [wear]
a pair of pants

치마를 입다
put on [wear] a skirt

~ 지퍼를 올리다
zip up ~

벨트를 매다
wear a belt

양말을 신다
put on [wear] some socks

넥타이를 매다
put on [wear] a tie

넥타이를 고쳐 매다
fix [straighten] one's tie

SENTENCES TO USE

치마부터 입어야 해요? 아니면 스타킹 먼저 신어야 해요?
Do I have to put on a skirt first? or stockings first?

바지 지퍼 올리는 것 잊지 마세요.　　　　Don't forget to zip up your pants.

바지 흘러내리기 전에 벨트를 매세요.　　　Please wear a belt before your pants roll down.

넥타이를 맬 때마다 전 불편해요.　　　　I feel uncomfortable whenever I wear a tie.

거울 보고 넥타이 좀 고쳐 매요.　　　　　Look into the mirror and fix your tie.

장롱/서랍을 뒤지다
rummage through one's
wardrobe / drawer

~ 단추를 잠그다
button (up) ~

~ 단추를 풀다
unbutton ~

장갑을 끼다
put on [wear]
one's gloves

가방을 챙기다
pack one's backpack

신발을 신다
put on [wear] one's shoes

불을 전부 끄다
turn off all the lights

문을 닫고 잠그다
close the door and lock it

집 밖으로 나가다, 집을 나서다
leave [get out of]
the house

SENTENCES TO USE

서랍 좀 그만 뒤적거려요! 당신 양말 여기 있잖아요.
Stop rummaging through your drawer! Your socks are right here.

아이들은 종종 셔츠 단추를 채우는 데 어려움을 겪습니다.
Children frequently have trouble buttoning up their shirt.

해변에서는 신발을 신을 필요가 없어요.
We don't have to wear shoes on the beach.

문 닫고 잠그기 전에 반드시 불을 다 꺼 주세요.
Make sure to turn off all the lights before closing and locking the door.

청소하게 아침에 집에서 나가 주시겠어요?
Do you mind leaving the house in the morning, so I can clean up?

CHAPTER

2

집안 일

HOUSEWORK

설거지하다
do the dishes

식탁을 치우다
clear the table

부엌을 싹 치우다
clean up the kitchen

방을 정돈하다
tidy up the room

방을 환기하다
air out [ventilate]
the room

물건을 치우다
put one's things
away

가구의 먼지를 털다
dust
the furniture

청소기로 바닥을 청소하다
vacuum
the floor

창문을 닦다
wipe the window

바닥을 대걸레로 닦다
mop the floor

변기/세면대/욕조를 박박 문질러 닦다
scrub the toilet / sink / bathtub

SENTENCES TO USE

식탁 치운 후에는 설거지를 하세요.　　　　Do the dishes after clearing the table.

집안 일을 안 도울 거라면, 최소한 네 방은 정리할 수 있어야지!
If you are not going to help around the house, you can at least tidy up your room!

네 장난감 치워라. 안 그럼 다 갖다 버릴 거야.
Put your toys away, or I will just throw them away.

청소기로 바닥 돌리기 전에 가구 먼지부터 털어요.
Let's dust the furniture before we vacuum the floor.

이 화장실 너무 더럽네요! 솔질한 지 얼마나 됐어요?
This bathroom is so dirty! How long has it been since you scrubbed it?

곰팡이를 제거하다
clean off [remove]
the mold

쓰레기를 내다 버리다
take out the trash
[garbage]

재활용 쓰레기를 분리 수거하다
separate [sort] the recyclable
waste [recyclables]

마당을 쓸다
sweep the yard

정원의 잡초를 뽑다
weed the garden

청소 대행 서비스를 예약하다/부르다
book / call a
cleaning service

물건을 정리하다
organize one's things

냉장고 청소를 하다
clean out the fridge,
clean the refrigerator

로봇청소기가 바닥 청소를 하다
a robot vacuum cleans
the floor

SENTENCES TO USE

네가 하는 유일한 집안 일이 쓰레기 내다 버리는 거였는데 넌 그걸 안 했어.
Your only chore was to take out the trash and you didn't do it.

환경에 도움이 되게 재활용 쓰레기를 분리하는 게 필수적입니다.
It is imperative to separate the recyclables to help the environment.

저는 집 밖에서 일을 많이 해서 정기적으로 청소 대행 서비스를 예약합니다.
I regularly book a cleaning service, since I work outside the house a lot.

이런! 휴가 가기 전에 냉장고 청소를 안 했다고요?
Oh no! You didn't clean out the fridge before you left for your vacation?

친구가 집들이 선물로 바닥 청소용 로봇청소기를 가지고 왔어요.
My friend brought a robot vacuum as a housewarming gift to clean the floor.

세탁물을 (색상별로/직물별로) 분류하다
sort out the laundry
(by color / fabric)

셔츠를 빨기 전에 물에 담그다
soak the shirt in water before washing,
pre-soak the shirt before washing

세탁기에 빨랫감을 넣다
put the laundry
in the washing machine

세탁기에 섬유유연제를 넣다
add the fabric softener
into the washing machine

마르라고 빨래를 넣다
hang the laundry
up to dry

빨래를 건조기에 넣다/돌리다
put the laundry in the dryer /
tumble dry the laundry

SENTENCES TO USE

세탁하기 전에 모두가 색깔별로 빨래를 분류해야 합니다.
Everyone needs to sort out their laundry by color before washing them.

스웨터는 줄어들기 때문에 건조기에 넣으면 안 됩니다.
Sweaters should not be put in the dryer because it will shrink.

옷을 개다
fold the clothes

옷을 다림질하다
iron the clothes

옷을 정리하다
organize clothes

옷장을 다시 정리하다
rearrange one's wardrobe

옷을 세탁소에 맡기다
take one's clothes to the
cleaner's [dry cleaner's]

옷을 세탁소에서 찾아오다
pick up one's clothes from
the cleaner's [dry cleaner's]

스팀 다리미/의류 관리기(스타일러)로 옷을 관리하다
take care of one's clothes with
a standing steam iron / a steam closet

피터는 주말에 자기 셔츠를 모두 직접 다림질합니다.
Peter irons all of his shirts himself on the weekend.

저는 봄마다 옷장을 다시 정리하는 습관이 있습니다.
I have a habit of rearranging my wardrobe every spring.

전 의류 관리기(스타일러)로 제 모든 니트 의류들을 관리해요.
I take care of all my knit wears with my steam closet.

A   자기야, 봄맞이 대청소하기 딱 좋은
　　 날씨다.
　　 ▶ Honey, it's a perfect day for
　　 spring cleaning today.

B   그래, 집이 지저분한데 오늘 한번
　　 윤이 반질반질 나게 치워 보자고.
　　 ● Sure, let's make this dirty
　　 house look spick and span.

A   일단 내가 청소기로 바닥 밀면
　　 자기가 대걸레로 깨끗이 닦아.
　　 ▶ You can mop the floor clean
　　 once I vacuum the floor.

B   알겠어. 그전에 침대랑 옷장에
　　 널브러져 있는 해진 빨랫감부터
　　 치워야 할 것 같은데.
　　 ● Okay. Before that, I think we
　　 should take care of the worn
　　 clothes all over the bed and
　　 the closet.

A   빨래 다 모아서 세탁기에 세제랑
　　 섬유유연제 붓고 넣어 줘.
　　 ▶ Let's collect all the laundry,
　　 put it in the washing machine
　　 with some detergent and
　　 fabric softener.

B   이불 빨래는 빨래방 가서 할 거지?
　　 ● Are we going to wash
　　 our comforters at the coin
　　 laundry?

A   응. 이불은 크잖아. 그래서 거기서
　　 돌리고 바로 건조기로 말릴 거야.
　　 ▶ Yes, the comforters are big.
　　 So, I am going to wash it there
　　 and use the dryer as well.

B   와, 먼지가 엄청나네! 창문 열고
　　 먼지부터 털어야겠어.
　　 ● Wow, there is a lot of dust!
　　 I'm going to open the window
　　 and dust it off.

A   그래. 그다음에 청소기 돌리는 게
　　 좋겠어.
　　 ▶ Yeah, I'd better vacuum after
　　 that.

B   빨래 마른 거 다 개서 옷장에
　　 집어넣을까?
　　 ● Should I fold all the dry
　　 laundry and put it in the
　　 closet?

A   응, 그런데 마른 수건은 화장실에 놓아야 해.

▶ Yes, but the dried towels should be put in the bathroom.

B   쓰레기는 다 분리 수거해서 바깥에다 내놓자.

● Let's separate all the trash and put it outside.

(한 시간 후 In an hour)

A   와! 집이 아주 깨끗해졌네. 수고 많았어.

▶ Wow! Our house is so clean. Well done.

B   자기도.

● You too, honey!

집 관리

공과금을 내다
pay one's (utility) bills

가계부를 기록하다
keep records of household
expenses, use an account book

난방을 켜다/끄다
turn on / off the heater

가습기를 켜다/끄다
turn on / off the
humidifier

제습기를 켜다/끄다
turn on / off the
dehumidifier

가전제품을 렌탈하다
rent a home
appliance

집을 수리하다
repair one's house

집 인테리어를 새로 하다
renovate [redecorate]
one's house

벽난로/샤워 부스를 설치하다
install a fireplace /
a shower stall [booth]

시공업자를 부르다
call a constructor

수리공을 부르다
call a repairman

SENTENCES TO USE

가스 요금을 안 내면 요리를 할 수 없을 거예요.
You need to pay your gas bills or you won't be able to cook.

팸은 가계부를 꼼꼼하게 기록합니다.
Pam is meticulous in keeping records of household expenses.

여기 좀 습하네요! 가습기는 끄고 제습기를 켜도록 해요.
It's humid in here! Let's turn off the humidifier and turn on the dehumidifier.

릴리는 화장실을 넓게 쓰게 욕조를 없애고 샤워 부스를 설치할 계획입니다.
Lily plans to remove the tub and install a shower stall for a spacious bathroom.

전 시공업자를 불러서 집 인테리어를 새로 하고 벽난로를 설치하려고 해요.
I am going to call a constructor to renovate my house and install a fireplace.

정원에서 허브를 키우다
grow herbs
in the garden

배선 공사를 하다
wire the cables,
connect the wires

도배하다
put up [install]
wallpaper

전구를 갈다
change [replace]
a light-bulb

수도관을 교체하다
replace water pipes

타일을 교체하다
replace the tile,
retile ~

공기청정기를 사용하다
use an air purifier

~을 수리받다,
(전문업자가) ~을 수리하다
have [get] ~ fixed

식물/꽃/채소에 물을 주다
water the plants / flowers /
vegetables

~를 다시
페인트칠하다
repaint ~

신발장을 정리하다
arrange one's shoe rack
[shoe closet]

SENTENCES TO USE

여자도 전구 갈 줄 압니다.
Women know how to change the light-bulb too.

건물 내 수도관 교체 작업은 시간이 오래 걸리는 일입니다.
Replacing water pipes in a building is a time-consuming job.

화장실의 깨진 타일들을 교체하는 데 얼마나 걸릴까요?
How long will it take to replace the broken tiles in the bathroom?

장마철 되기 전에 서둘러 지붕을 고치자고요.
Let's be hasty and get the roof fixed before the rainy season.

그 창틀은 교체한 후에 다시 칠해야 합니다.
That window frame is to be repainted after it's replaced.

A 인테리어 공사를 어떻게
해드릴까요?
▶ How would you like your
interior done?

B 일단, 이쪽 벽을 헐어내서 거실
크기를 더 키울 거고요.
● First, I want this wall torn for
a bigger living room.

테라스와 거실 사이에 유리로 된
미닫이 문을 설치할 거예요.
● And I also want a glass
sliding door installed between
the terrace and the living
room.

A 네, 장식장은 오른쪽 코너에
제작해 드리면 되겠죠?
▶ Okay. And you want the
cabinet on the right corner,
right?

B 네, 그런데 장식장을 에어컨이랑
너무 가깝지 않게 설치해 주세요.
● That's right. But please
install the cabinet not too
close to the air conditioner.

A 부엌은 어떻게 해드릴까요?
▶ How about the kitchen?

B 싱크대를 흰색 톤의 친환경 재료
제품으로 교체해 주세요.
● Please replace the sink with
a white-toned eco-friendly
material.

A 식탁은 아일랜드 식탁으로 벽에
붙여서 제작해 드리면 되죠?
▶ Should I build the island
table attached to the wall?

B 네, 식탁 표면은 대리석으로
제작해 주시고요.
● Yes, please. And make the
countertop out of marble.

A 화장실은 샤워 부스를 설치하고
변기를 교체하면 될까요?
▶ Should I install a shower
stall and replace the toilet in
the bathroom?

B 네, 추가로 제가 알려 드린 모양으로
타일 시공하는 것 잊지 마시고요.
● Yes, and additionally, don't
forget to construct the tiles in
the shape I mentioned.

A 알겠습니다. 벽지와 조명은
   어떻게 할까요?
   ▶ No problem. What about the
   wallpaper and the lighting?

B 벽지는 W2103 모델로 해 주시고
   거실에 샹들리에를 달 거예요.
   ● Use the W2103 model for
   the wallpaper and a chandelier
   will be hung in the living
   room.

   나머지는 일반 30W LED 램프로
   해 주세요.
   ● Please use regular 30W LED
   lamps for the rest.

A 알겠습니다. 그 밖에 더 필요한 건
   없으세요?
   ▶ Okay. Do you need anything
   else?

B 네, (시공하는 데) 시간이 얼마나
   걸리고 비용이 얼마나 들까요?
   ● Yup. How long will it take
   and how much will it cost?

A 공사 기간과 비용 견적 정리해서
   이메일로 보내 드리겠습니다.
   ▶ I will send you an email after
   organizing the estimate of the
   construction period and the
   cost.

모유 수유/분유 수유를 하다
breastfeed /
bottle-feed (one's baby)

이유식을 먹이다
feed baby food

기저귀를 갈다
change one's diaper

아기용품을 소독하다
disinfect baby
supplies

걸음마 훈련을 하다
train one's steps,
teach a baby to walk

배변 훈련을 하다
potty-train [toilet
train] one's child

아이와 교감하다
interact with
one's child

아이를 유모차에 태우다
put a child in a
stroller

아이와 산책하다
take a walk with
one's child

자장가를 불러주다
sing a lullaby

보채는 아이를 달래다
soothe a fussy [an
upset] child

~를 재우다/~를 낮잠 재우다
put ~ to sleep /
put ~ down for a nap

SENTENCES TO USE

아기들은 고형 음식을 먹기 전에 보통 모유 수유를 하거나 분유 수유를 합니다.
Babies are usually breastfed or bottlefed before eating solid foods.

어떤 엄마들은 아기가 만지는 모든 걸 소독하는 것에 매우 까다롭습니다.
Some mothers are very particular about disinfecting everything her baby touches.

유치원에 가기 전에 아이에게 배변 훈련을 시키는 것이 중요합니다.
It is important to potty-train your child before they go to kindergarten.

저는 유모차에 아기 태우고 같이 산책하는 걸 좋아합니다.
I like to put my baby in a stroller and take a walk with him.

애가 오늘따라 많이 보채는 것 같은데, 낮잠을 재우는 게 어때요?
He seems very fussy today, why don't you put him down for a nap?

~를 어린이집에 데려가다
take ~ to a
daycare center

~를 유치원에 보내다
send ~ to
kindergarten

키즈카페에 가다
go to a kids cafe

키즈카페에서 아이와 놀다
play with a child
at a kids cafe

육아 정보를 공유하다
share parenting
information

육아 상담을 받다
receive childcare
counseling

(아이에게) 예방 접종을 맞히다
get one's child
vaccinated

(아이) 정기 검진을 받다
have [get] a regular
checkup (for one's child)

아이의 식사를/간식을 준비하다
prepare a child's meal /
snack

잘한 행동을 칭찬하다
praise one's
good behavior

~를 훈육하다
discipline ~

SENTENCES TO USE

제 딸은 제가 어린이집에만 데려가면 오열하곤 했습니다.
My daughter used to wail when I took her to the daycare center.

키즈카페에서 아이와 놀 때마다 지쳐 나가떨어지는 사람이 저예요.
Whenever I play with a child at a kids cafe, I am the one who gets exhausted.

엄마는 아이랑 키즈카페에 가서 아이들이 노는 동안 육아 정보를 공유할 수 있습니다.   A mother can go to a kids cafe
with her child and share parenting information while the kids play.

아들이 제대로 성장하지 못한다는 생각이 들면 육아 상담을 받아보세요.
You should receive childcare counseling if you feel like your son seems underdeveloped.

정기 검진을 받고 아이에게 예방 접종을 맞히는 것이 필수입니다.
It is vital to get a regular checkup and get one's child vaccinated.

반려동물에게 사료(먹이)를 주다
feed one's pet, feed food to
one's pet, give food to one's pet

배변 패드를 깔다
lay out pads
[potty-pads]

배변 패드를 갈아주다
change dirty pads
[potty-pads]

목줄을 채우다
put on a leash

입마개를 채우다
put a muzzle on

비닐봉지에 반려동물의 변을 담다
pack the pet poop in a plastic bag

SENTENCES TO USE

짐은 나이 먹은 자기 고양이에게 늘 고급 유기농 동물 사료를 먹여요.
Jim always feeds high-grade organic pet food to his elderly cat.

반려동물 산책시키기 전에 목줄 채우는 것 잊지 마세요.
Don't forget to put on a leash before taking your pet out for a walk.

개가 길에서 뭔지 주워 먹으려고 하면, 주인은 개에게 입마개를 씌워야 합니다.
If a dog tries to eat anything on the street, the owner must put a muzzle on the dog.

MP3 0 1 7

반려동물 용품점에서 물건을 사다
buy things at the pet shop

동물 미용실에 가다
go to the pet groomer

~를 목욕시키다
give a bath to ~

동물병원에서 검사를 받다
visit the vet, get a check-up at the vet

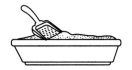

고양이 변기통을 청소하다
clean the litter box

던지고 물어오기 놀이를 하다
play fetch

고양이 세 마리를 목욕시키는 건 너무 피곤한 일입니다.
It is exhausting to give baths to 3 cats.

우리 개랑 3시간 동안 던지고 물어오기 놀이를 하면 전 녹초가 됩니다.
I am worn out after playing fetch with my dog for 3 hours.

CHAPTER

이동

TRANSPORTATION

UNIT 1 이동

~를 (차에) 태우러 가다
pick (somebody) up

아이를 학교에 내려주다
drop one's child
off at school

걸어서 출근하다
go to work
on foot

지나가다 이웃을 만나
인사를 나누다
run into one's
neighbors and say hello

횡단보도에서 길을 건너다
walk across the street
at a crosswalk

신호등이 바뀌기를 기다리다
wait for the light to
change

육교를 건너다
cross [go over] the
pedestrian overpass

지하도를 통해 가다
go through the
underpass

버스 정류장/지하철역으로 이동하다
move [get] to the bus /
subway station

교통카드를 구입하다
buy a transit card

교통카드를 충전하다
recharge a transit card

SENTENCES TO USE

리 씨는 이번 업무 회의에 오기 전에 아이를 학교에 내려줘야 합니다.
Mr. Leigh has to drop his kid off at school before he comes to this business meeting.

주디는 횡단보도를 건너기 전에 이웃을 만났습니다.
Judy ran into her neighbor before she crossed the crosswalk.

그는 한참 동안 신호가 바뀌기를 기다렸습니다.
He has been waiting for the light to change for a while.

저는 어렸을 때 육교 건너는 걸 아주 싫어했고, 지금도 그렇습니다.
I hated going over the pedestrian overpass as a kid, and I still do.

교통카드 충전하는 것을 잊어서 다음 열차를 타야 했어요.
I had to take the next train because I forgot to recharge my transit card.

50

길을 따라 걷다
walk along the street

지나가는 사람에게 길을 묻다
ask a passerby for
directions

길을 안내하다
show [guide]
the way

앞으로 쭉 가다
go [walk] straight
(forward)

~를 지나가다
go pass ~

~에서 왼쪽으로 돌다
turn left at ~

~를 지나서 오른쪽으로 돌다
turn right after ~

지도를 따라 이동하다
follow along the map

도착 시간을 확인하다
check the arrival time

목적지에 도착하다
arrive at the destination

버스 정류장에서 줄 서서 기다리다
wait in line at the bus stop

SENTENCES TO USE

교회에 도착할 때까지 그냥 계속 직진하세요.
Just keep walking straight until you arrive at the church.

소방서 지나서 횡단보도에서 우회전하세요.
Go pass the fire station and turn right at the crosswalk.

길을 잘 모르겠으면(길치라면), 계속 지도를 따라서 가세요!
If you are bad with directions, just keep following along the map!

내가 차로 너 데리러 갈 수 있게 도착 시간 확인해 줄 수 있어?
Could you check your arrival time so I can go pick you up?

저는 러시아워 때마다 버스 정류장에서 줄 서서 기다려야 합니다.
I have to wait in line at the bus stop every rush hour.

A 안녕하세요. ABC 호텔에 가려고
하는데 어떻게 가는지 알려 주시겠
어요?
▶ Hello. I'm trying to get to
the ABC Hotel, could you tell
me how to get there?

B 아, 네. 잠시만요. 앱으로 확인하고
알려 드릴게요.
● Ah yes, just a moment. I'll
check on my phone app and
let you know.

A 네, 감사합니다.
▶ Okay, thanks.

B 이 길로 쭉 200미터 걸어가시면
XYZ 마트가 나와요. 거기서 오른쪽
길로 들어가시면 장난감 상가 골목
이 나오는데요. 그 골목 끝까지 가셔
서 왼쪽으로 꺾으면 이스턴 유니언
역 1번 출구가 있어요.
● If you walk 200 meters
straight this way, you will
find the XYZ Mart. If you turn
right from there, you will find
the alley of the toy stores. Go
to the end of that alley and
turn left, you will find exit 1 of
Eastern Union Station.

A 이스턴 유니언역에서 지하철을 타
면 되나요?
▶ Should I take the subway at
Eastern Union Station?

B 네, 제임스 타운 방향 1호선 지하철
을 타시고 제이드 파크역에서 내려
서 5번 출구로 나가세요.
● Yes, take the subway Line 1
towards James Town, get off
at Jade Park Station, and go to
exit 5.

거기서 출구 반대 방향으로 돌아서
50미터쯤 가면 버스 정류장이
있어요.
● There is a bus station about
50 meters away from the
opposite direction of the exit.

정류장에서 123번 버스 타고 4 정거
장 가서 내리세요.
● Take the bus number 123
and get off after 4 stations.

버스 정류장 앞 횡단보도를 건너서
팜스퀘어 시장 방면으로 5분 정도
걸어가세요.
● Cross the crosswalk in
front of the bus stop and walk
toward Farmsquare Market for
about 5 minutes.

거기서 소방서가 나오면 왼쪽 길로
들어가셔서 양 갈래 길이 나오면 오
른쪽 길로 가세요.
● When you get to the fire
station, turn left, and go
towards the right road when
the road splits.

30미터쯤 더 걸어가시면 ABC 호텔
이 있을 거예요.
● Walk for about 30 more
meters and there will be the
ABC Hotel.

A 생각보다 길이 훨씬 더 복잡하네요.
그냥 택시 타고 가야겠어요.
▶ The way there is a lot more
complicated than I thought. I
think I'll just take a taxi.

B 네, 그게 훨씬 더 편하실 거예요.
● Yeah, that would be much
more convenient.

택시 기사에게 주소 알려 주시고 내
비게이션 찍고 가 달라고 하세요.
● Just give the location to the
driver and use the navigation
system.

A 친절하게 알려 주셔서 감사합니다.
▶ Thank you for your kindness.

버스 & 지하철

차를 몰고 출근하다
drive one's car
to work

자전거를 타고 ~에 가다
ride a bike to ~

* carpool은
명사로도 쓰임.

카풀을 하다
carpool,
use a car pool

버스를/지하철을 타다
take [ride] the bus /
subway

교통카드를 단말기에 대다
touch [scan] the transit
card to the card reader

손잡이를 잡다
hold on to a strap

스마트폰을 가지고 놀다
play on one's smartphone

좌석에 앉아서 졸다
doze off on the seat

임산부/노인에게 자리를 양보하다
offer one's seat to a pregnant
lady / an elderly person

다른 교통수단으로 갈아타다
transfer to a different
means of transportation

빈 좌석에 앉다
sit on an
empty seat

SENTENCES TO USE

잭슨은 보통 차를 운전해서 출근하는데, 건강해지기 위해 자전거를 타기로 했습니다.
Jackson usually drives his car to work, but he decided to ride his bike to get healthy.

제 상사가 직장 동료들을 위해 카풀을 마련했습니다. My boss arranged a carpool for colleagues at work.

많은 사람들이 퇴근 후에 좌석에 앉아서 좁니다. A lot of people doze off on the seat after work

차가 막혀서 전 지하철로 갈아타야 했습니다.
I had to transfer to the subway because of the traffic jam.

버스에서 빈자리에 앉았는데, 다음 정류장에서 어르신께 자리를 양보했습니다.
I sat on an empty seat on the bus, but I offered my seat to an elderly at the next stop.

통로에 서다
stand on
the aisle

버스에서 정차 버튼을 누르다
press the 'stop' button
on the bus

버스/지하철에서 내리다
get off the bus /
subway

개찰구를 빠져나오다
come out through
the turnstile

* '나오다'는
go out으로도
표현.

~번 출구로 나오다
get out
through exit

정기권을 구매하다/사용하다
buy / use a commutation
ticket [card]

대중교통을 이용하다
use public [mass]
transportation

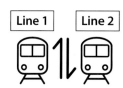

~에서 2호선으로 환승하다
transfer to Line
Number 2 at ~

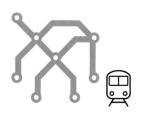

버스/지하철 노선도를 확인하다
check the bus / subway (route) map

버스/열차를 놓치다
miss a bus / a train

시간표를 확인하다
check the timetable

SENTENCES TO USE

버스 안이 너무 붐벼서 미아는 통로에 서 있을 수밖에 없었습니다.
The bus was so packed that Mia had no choice but to stand on the aisle.

버스에서 내리기 전에 정차 버튼을 눌러야 합니다.
You need to press the stop button before getting off the bus.

빅토리아역에서 몇 번 출구로 나가야 하는지 도대체 알 수가 없습니다.
It is impossible to find which exit I need to go out at Victoria Station.

평일에는 대중교통을 이용하는 것이 현명합니다.
It is wise to use public transportation during weekdays.

버스 놓치지 않으려면 시간표를 확인해 보세요.
Check the timetable if you don't want to miss the bus.

3 택시

스마트폰으로 택시를 찾다
look for a taxi [a cab] on the phone

앱으로 택시를 부르다
call [request] a taxi [a cab] with a phone app

(길거리에서) 택시를 잡다
grab [get] a taxi [a cab]

택시에 타다
get in [into] a taxi [a cab]

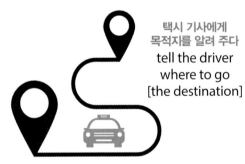

택시 기사에게
목적지를 알려 주다
tell the driver
where to go
[the destination]

창밖을 바라보다
look out the window

SENTENCES TO USE

날씨가 안 좋을 때마다 앱으로 택시 부르는 게 시간이 오래 걸립니다.
It takes a long time to request a taxi with a phone app whenever the weather is bad.

비 오기 시작하잖아! 나 그냥 나가서 택시 잡을래.
It's starting to rain! I'm just going to grab a taxi.

켄은 멀미 때문에 창밖을 바라봐야 합니다.
Ken has to look out the window due to his motion sickness.

스마트폰으로 뉴스를 보다
watch the news on one's phone

스마트폰으로 주식 시황을 확인하다
check the stock market on one's phone

택시 기사와 이야기를 나누다
have a conversation
[converse] with
the taxi [cab] driver

미터기 요금을 확인하다
check the price on the meter

현금으로/카드로 결제하다
pay in cash / with a card

택시에서 내리다
get out of [off]
the taxi [cab]

앱에 탑승 서비스 리뷰를 남기다
give [leave] a review on the app
for the service

택시 기사와 대화하는 게 제겐 매우 어색합니다.
Having a conversation with the cab driver is very awkward for me.

대니는 현금이 부족해서 미터기 요금을 계속 확인했어요.
Danny kept checking the price on the meter because he was short on cash.

4 운전

전자키로 차문을 열다
open the car with the electronic key

차에 타다
get in the car

안전벨트를 매다
buckle [fasten] the seat belt

차에 시동을 걸다
start the car

백미러/사이드미러를 조정하다
adjust the rear-view mirrors /
side-view mirrors

후진 기어를 걸다
shift into reverse

차를 주차장 밖으로 빼다
get the car out of the
parking lot

횡단보도 앞에서 멈추다
stop in front of the
crosswalk

SENTENCES TO USE

드라이브 나가기 전에 안전벨트를 매는 것이 중요합니다.
It's vital to buckle the seat belt before going out for a drive.

후진 기어 걸기 전에 사이드미러를 조정하세요.
Adjust the side-view mirrors before shifting into reverse.

어린이 보호구역에서 속도를 줄이다
slow down at the children
protection zone

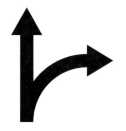

교차로에서 좌회전/우회전하다
turn left / right at the intersection

유턴하다
make [take]
a U-turn

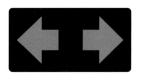

좌측/우측/비상 깜빡이를 켜다
turn on the left-turn / right-turn /
emergency signal

후면 주차하다
back-in park one's car

전면 주차하다
head-in park one's car

어린이 보호구역에서 속도를 줄이지 않으면 벌금이 셉니다.
The fine is high for not slowing down at the children protection zone.

우회전하기 전에 항상 보행자가 없는지 확인하세요
Always make sure there are no pedestrians before you turn right.

엄마가 불법 유턴으로 딱지를 떼었습니다.
My mother got a ticket for making an illegal U-turn.

차를 갓길에 정차하다
pull the car over to the shoulder
[edge of the road]

톨게이트에서 도로 이용료를 내다
pay the toll
at the tollgate

* 우리나라의 하이패스 같은 시스템을 보통 Electronic Toll Collection (ETC)이라고 함.

톨게이트에서 하이패스를 통과하다
go through the Hi-Pass at the tollgate

66번 국도를 달리다
drive on Route 66

와이퍼를 켜다
turn on the wipers

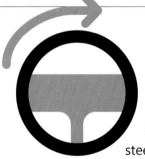

핸들을 틀다
steer the wheel,
turn the steering wheel

SENTENCES TO USE

호텔로 가려면 2번 국도로 달리다가 톨게이트 지나서 빠지면 됩니다.
To get to the hotel, drive on Route 2 and exit after the tollgate.

비 오네! 와이퍼 켜고 김 서림 방지 버튼 눌러 줘.
It's raining! Please turn on the wipers and press the demister button.

김 서림 방지 버튼을 누르다
press the demister button

창문을/선루프를 열고 환기하다
open the window / sun-roof to air out

주유를 하다
refuel one's car, fill (up) with gas

주유기에서 결제를 하다
pay at the gas pump

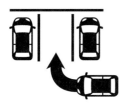

주차장에 차를 주차하다
park the car in the parking lot

* put 대신 shift to 로도 사용 가능.

기어를 P에 놓고 차에서 내리다
put the car in park and get off

신용카드를 깜박해서 차에 기름을 넣을 수가 없었어요.
I forgot my credit card, so I couldn't refuel my car.

제이크는 주말마다 빈 주차장에 주차된 자기 차 손 세차하는 걸 좋아합니다.
Jake loves to handwash his car parked at the vacant parking lot on the weekends.

A 자, 너도 운전면허증 땄으니까 밖에 나가서 도로 주행 연습을 해 보자.
▶ Since you got your driver's license, let's go out and practice your driving skills on the road.

B 실제 도로 운전은 처음 하는 건데 괜찮을까?
● It's my first-time driving on the actual road, will it be okay?

A 걱정하지 마. 내가 조수석에 타서 안전하게 운전하도록 계속 잔소리 할 거니까. 하하.
▶ Don't worry, I'll keep nagging you to drive safely in the passenger seat. Haha.

자, 일단 차에 타서 벨트 매고 시동을 걸어.
▶ Now, get in the car, buckle up, and start the car.

후진 기어 걸고 차를 뒤로 빼고 전진 기어로 바꾸고 액셀러레이터를 살짝 밟아 주면서 천천히 출발해.
▶ Put the gear on reverse, pull back, put the gear on drive, step on the accelerator and drive slowly.

B 휴, 브레이크를 너무 세게 밟으니까 차가 흔들리네.
● Phew, the car is shaking because I'm hitting the brakes too hard.

A 괜찮아. 처음엔 다 그래.
▶ It's okay, it's like that at first.

브레이크 살짝 밟고 안전거리 유지하며 가는 거야.
▶ Step on the brakes lightly and keep a safe distance.

B 신호등이 노란색인데 그냥 빨리 지나갈까?
● The traffic light is yellow, should I quickly pass by?

A 아니, 우리 앞의 차가 밀려서 따라가다가 교차로 가운데에서 길을 막을 수도 있으니까 멈추자.
▶ No, let's stop because the car in front of us might get stuck and block the road in the middle of the intersection.

B 어린이 보호구역에서는 아무래도 운전하는 게 더 조심스러워지네.
● I'm becoming more careful driving in child protection zones.

A 맞아. 시속 30킬로미터 이하로 운전 해야 하고 아이들이 갑자기 튀어나 올 수 있으니까 더 주의해야 해.
▶ That's right. You have to drive less than 30km/h, and you have to be more careful because children can jump out of nowhere.

B 여기서 유턴해야 하나?
● Should I make a U-turn here?

A 응, 지도 앱이 좌회전 신호 받을 때 유턴하라고 하니까 신호 뜰 때까지 기다렸다가 유턴해.
▶ Yes, the GPS app is telling me to make a U-turn when I get a left turn signal, so wait until the signal comes up and make a U-turn.

B 좌회전하려고 하는데 비보호 표지판이 있으면 어떻게 하지?
● If I want to turn left and there's an unprotected sign, what should I do?

A 반대편에서 차 오는지 잘 보고 오는 차가 없을 때 좌회전해.
▶ Check to see if the car is coming out from the other side and turn left when there is none coming.

B 어, 갑자기 비가 오네. 안개도 끼고 말이야. 갑자기 시야가 좁아졌어.
● Oh, it's raining all of the sudden, and it's getting foggy, too. My vision is suddenly narrowed.

A 와이퍼 최대치로 켜고, 비상등 켠 다음에 김 서림 방지 버튼 눌러.
▶ Switch the wiper to the maximum, turn on the emergency light, and press the demister button.

B 휴~ 거의 다 왔다. 차는 어디다 댈까?
● Phew ~ We're almost there. Where should I park the car?

A 저기 저 차 앞에 주차하면 되겠다.
▶ You can park in front of the car over there.

운전 처음 하는 것 치고는 아주 잘했어. 수고했어.
▶ You did a great job for the first-time driving. Good job.

(다른 사람이) 세차하다
have [get] one's
car washed

자동 세차를 하다
go through an
automatic car wash

사이드미러를 접고
자동 세차를 하다
fold the side-view mirror
for (an automatic) car wash

손 세차를 하다
wash one's car
by hand

헝겊으로 차의 물기를 닦다
dry one's car with a cloth [a rag]

진공청소기로 차량 내부를 청소하다
vacuum the interior of one's car

SENTENCES TO USE

저는 주말마다 손 세차를 하곤 했습니다.
I used to wash my car by hand every weekend.

네가 어질러 놓았으니 내 차 내부는 네가 진공청소기로 청소해야지.
You should vacuum the interior of my car since you made the mess.

바닥 매트를 청소하다
clean the floor mats

계기판을 닦다
wipe off the dashboard

타이어에 공기를 주입하다
pump air into a tire

워셔액을 보충하다
add [refill] washer fluid [liquid]

냉각수를 보충하다/교체하다
add / change coolant

차에 왁스 칠을 하다
wax one's car

제나는 남편이 헝겊으로 차 물기를 닦는 동안 계기판을 닦았습니다.
Jenna wiped off the dashboard while her husband dried the car with a rag.

네 타이어가 납작해진 게 보여! 타이어에 바람 넣어 줘.
I can see that your tires are flat! Please pump air into your tires.

고등학교 때 선생님이 워셔액 보충하는 법을 가르쳐 주셨어요.
My teacher taught me how to refill washer fluid in high school.

(다른 사람이) 차를 점검하다
have [get] one's car
checked [inspected]

~의 수리 견적을 받다
get [receive] a repair
estimate for ~

(다른 사람이) 고장 난 차를 고치다
have [get] one's car
repaired [fixed]

**(다른 사람이) 엔진 오일/브레이크 오일을
점검하다/교체하다**
have [get] the engine oil / brake oil
checked / changed

(다른 사람이) 에어 필터를 교체하다
have one's car
air filter changed

타이어 상태를 확인하다
check the tires

(다른 사람이) 타이어를 점검하다/위치를 교체하다
have the tires checked / rotated

SENTENCES TO USE

찰리는 그의 차 수리 견적서를 받아보고 거의 기절할 뻔했습니다.
Charlie almost fainted when he received the estimate for his car repair.

좋든 싫든 간에 경고등이 켜지면 엔진 오일을 교체해야 합니다.
Whether you like it or not, you have to get the engine oil changed if the warning light is on.

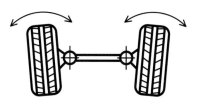

휠 얼라인먼트를 받다
get a wheel alignment,
get the wheels aligned

(다른 사람이) 와이퍼를 교체하다
have the wipers
[windshield wipers] changed

움푹 팬 곳을 펴다
straighten out a dent

차를 도장하다
paint one's car,
coat one's car with paint

(다른 사람이) 자동차 에어컨을 점검하다
have one's car air conditioner
checked

주기적으로 휠 얼라인먼트를 받는 것이 안전에 좋습니다.
Getting a wheel alignment regularly is good for safety.

이 움푹 팬 곳을 편 후에는 차 도장할 수 있을 거예요.
I should be able to paint the car after straightening out this dent.

네 차 에어컨에서 냄새나니까 점검 받아봐야 해!
You need to have your car air conditioner checked, because it smells!

CHAPTER

4

장소

PLACES

카페

카페에 가다, 카페에 들르다
visit [go to]
a café

마실 음료를 고르다
choose drinks
[beverages]

음료를 주문하다
order drinks
[beverages]

가판대에서 음료를 주문하다
order drinks from a kiosk

드라이브 스루로 주문하다
order on a drive-through [drive-thru]

음료 값을 계산하다
pay for the drinks

거스름돈을 받다
get change

현금 영수증 번호를 입력하다
enter in the number for a cash receipt

* 전화번호나
사업자번호로
현금영수증 적립할 수 있게
입력하는 것.

SENTENCES TO USE

시험 보러 가기 전에 카페에 가서 커피 한잔해요.
Let's go to the café and get some coffee before we head to our exam.

그는 주문한 것 값을 내고 거스름돈 받는 것을 잊었습니다.
He forgot to get change after he paid for his order.

할인 코드(프로모션 코드)를 입력하다
enter in a promotion code

포인트를 적립하다
earn loyalty [frequent-customer] points

포인트 사용을/적립을 깜빡하다
forget to use /
accumulate points

적립 카드에 스탬프를 찍다
get one's loyalty card
[frequent-customer card] stamped

모바일 쿠폰을/기프트 카드를 쓰다
use a mobile coupon [voucher] /
gift card

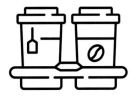

~을 테이크아웃하다
buy ~ for take-out,
order [get] ~ to go

음료수 값 내기 전에 할인 코드(프로모션 코드) 사용하는 것 잊지 마세요.
Don't forget to use the promotion code before paying for the drinks.

난 여기 적립 카드 없는데, 네 걸로 찍을래?
I don't have a loyalty card here. Would you like to get yours stamped?

생일 선물로 받은 모바일 기프트 카드가 있는데 그걸로 텀블러를 살 거예요.
I have a mobile gift card I got for my birthday, and I'm going to buy a tumbler with it.

컵에 홀더를 끼우다
put the cup holder
[sleeve] on

냅킨을 챙기다
get napkins

~에 시럽을 추가하다
add syrup to ~

자리를 잡다
get a table [seats]

사용한 머그잔과 쟁반을 반납하다
return the used mugs
and trays

셀프바를 이용하다
use the self-service
station

얼음이 담긴 컵을 하나 받다(얻다)
get a cup of ice

SENTENCES TO USE

주문하기 전에 자리 먼저 잡자.
Let's get a table first before we order.

우리 선생님은 커피에 시럽이나 설탕 추가하는 것 안 좋아하세요.
My teacher does not like syrup or sugar added to her coffee.

셀프바에서 음료에 넣을 계핏가루를 찾으실 수 있습니다.
You can find some cinnamon powder to put in your drink at the self-service station.

진동 벨을 받다
get the vibration bell [buzzer, pager]

전광판에서 번호를 확인하다
check the number on the electronic display

진동 벨이 울리면 주문한 음료를 받다
pick up the drinks
when the pager rings

우유 대신 두유로 바꿔 주문하다
order soy milk instead of
regular milk, replace regular
milk with soy milk

일반 우유 대신 저지방 우유로 바꿔 주문하다
order low-fat milk instead of regular milk,
replace regular milk with low-fat milk

디카페인 음료로 주문하다
order a decaffeinated drink,
order decaff

그녀는 유당 불내증이 있어서 주문할 때 일반 우유를 두유로 대체합니다.
She replaces regular milk with soy milk in all her orders, because she is lactose intolerant.
저는 저녁에는 항상 디카페인 저지방 라테를 주문합니다.
I always order decaff low-fat latte in the evening.

A 안녕하세요. 주문할게요.
▶ Hello. Can I order, please?

B 어서 오세요. 드시고 가세요,
가지고 가세요?
● Welcome. For here, or to
go?

A 먹고 가려고요. 따뜻한 아메리카노
연하게 한 잔이랑 아이스 카페라테
한 잔 주세요.
▶ For here. I would like a weak
hot americano and an iced
latte, please.

그리고 오븐에 구운 크림치즈
베이글 하나랑 치즈케이크
한 조각도요.
▶ And one oven-baked cream
cheese bagel and a piece of
cheesecake, too.

B 네, 따뜻한 아메리카노와
아이스 카페라테 사이즈는
어떻게 해드릴까요?
● Okay, what size would you
like for your hot americano
and iced latte?

A 아메리카노는 스몰 사이즈로,
카페라테는 미디엄으로 해 주세요.
▶ Small size for the americano
and a medium for the latte,
please.

B 카페 이용 손님은 머그잔으로
음료가 제공되고 이용 시간이
4시간으로 제한됩니다.

● Customers using our café
will be served drinks in mugs
and the usage time is limited
to 4 hours.

괜찮으세요?
● Would that be all right?

A 네. (카페라테) 우유는 저지방 우유로
해 주시고 위에 휘핑크림
올려 주시겠어요?
▶ That's perfect. Could you
replace the milk for low-fat
milk and add whipping cream
on top?

B 휘핑 크림은 1 달러 추가되는데
괜찮으세요?
● Whipping cream is an extra
dollar, is that okay?

A 네, 괜찮아요. 카드 여기 있습니다.
▶ That's good. Here is my card.

B 어, 카드가 오류라고 뜨는데 혹시
다른 카드로 결제하시겠어요?
● Oh no, this card has an
error. Could you pay with
another card?

A 그러면 모바일 상품권으로 할게요.
▶ Oh, then I will use my mobile gift card.

B 네, 12달러 결제되었습니다.
● Sure. 12 dollars was charged.

잔액 38달러는 나중에 사용하시면 되고요.
● 38 dollars is left in the balance for later use.

현금영수증 해드릴까요?
● Would you like a cash receipt?

A 네, 전화번호로 입력할게요.
▶ Yes, I'll use my phone number.

B 네, 손님. 여기 진동 벨 받으시고 진동 벨이 울리면 픽업 구역으로 오셔서 가져가시면 됩니다.
● Thank you. Here is your vibration bell, and you can come get your drinks at the pick-up zone once it buzzes.

더 필요한 건 없으세요?
● Do you need anything else?

A 아메리카노에 시럽 두 펌프 정도 넣어 주시고 냅킨 좀 주시겠어요?
▶ Could you add 2 pumps of syrup for the americano, and give me some napkins?

B 시럽과 냅킨은 셀프 바에 있습니다.
● Syrup and napkins are at the self-service station over there.

A 네, 감사합니다.
▶ Thank you very much.

COFFE
LATTE
MOCHA
ESPRESSO
MACCIATO   LEMONADE
CAPPUCCINO   TEA

2 주문 오류

... 대신 ~로 잘못 주문하다
order ~ instead of ...
by mistake

다른 사람 음료를/주문한 것을 가져오다
get someone else's drink / order

주문과 다른 음료가 나오다 (주문 착오)
get a different drink than one ordered,
mix up drinks, have an order mix up

결제를 취소하다
cancel payment

일부 금액을 환불받다
get a partial refund

잘못 계산하다
make a wrong
payment

기한 만료된 카드를 쓰다
use an invalid [expired] card

SENTENCES TO USE

이런, 실수로 뜨거운 차 대신 아이스티를 주문했어요.
Oh no, I ordered iced tea instead of hot tea by mistake.

리암은 주문 착오 때문에 카페 매니저와 실랑이를 벌여야 했습니다.
Liam had to argue with the cafe manager because of his order mix up.

엠마는 품절된 조각 케이크에 부분 환불을 받았습니다.
Emma got a partial refund for the sold out piece of cake.

카드 사용 불가
card service unavailable

신용카드 인식이 안 되다, 신용카드가 결제가 안 되다
be unable to read [use] a credit card,
one's card doesn't go through

결제 방식을 바꾸다
change payment
method

주문한 음료가 맛이 없어서 다른 음료로 재구매하다
buy [order] another drink because the
previous drink didn't taste good [was bad]

주문이 누락되다
an order is left out [missing]

키오스크 에러 때문에 주문 불가하다
be unable to order due to an error in the kiosk

어제 제 카드가 결제가 안 되더라고요. 만료되었나 봐요.
My card did not go through yesterday, maybe it's expired.

그 카페는 어제 키오스크 오류로 인해 현금만 받고 있었습니다.
That cafe was accepting only cash yesterday due to an error in the kiosk.

편의점에 가다
go to a convenience store

구급상자를 사다
buy a first-aid kit

~의 유통기한을 확인하다
check the expiration
date of ~

전자레인지에 즉석식품을 데우다
heat up instant food in the
microwave

할인 상품을 찾다
look for a
discounted product

종량제 봉투를 구입하다
buy a standard
garbage bag

SENTENCES TO USE

결제하기 전에 할인 상품의 유통기한을 확인해야 합니다.
You should check the expiration date of the discounted products before paying.

저는 어묵 꼬치를 먹기 전에 전자레인지에 데웁니다.
I heat up my fish cake skewers in the microwave before eating them.

편의점에서 복권을 사다
buy a lottery ticket
at a convenience store

나이 확인을 위해 신분증 검사를 하다
check one's ID for one's age

구입한 음식을
매장에서 먹다
eat one's food
at the store

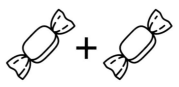

1+1 제품을 구매하다
buy a one-plus-one product,
buy one-get-one free

4캔 이상 구매 시 할인해 주는 맥주를 고르다
choose a beer with a discount on
purchases of more than four cans

편의점에서 복권 한 장을 사서 당첨될 확률이 얼마나 될까요?
What are the chances of buying a single lottery ticket at a convenience store and winning?

담배를 사려고 할 때 아르바이트생이 제 신분증을 확인했습니다.
A part-timer checked my ID when I tried to buy cigarettes.

컵라면, 매장에서 드실 거예요, 집에 가져가실 거예요?
Are you going to eat cup noodles at the store or take them home?

MP3 032

서점에 들르다
stop by a
bookstore

베스트셀러를 확인하다/찾다
check out / look for
the bestseller

책의 위치를 검색하다
search the location
of a book

책들을 비교하다
compare
books

책을 고르다
choose a
book

잡지를/책을 넘겨보다,
훑어보다
thumb [leaf] through
a magazine / a book

할인 쿠폰을 제시하다
show [give] a discount
coupon

온라인에서 결제한
책을 픽업하다
pick up a book
paid online

중고 서점에 가다
go to a secondhand
[used] bookstore

중고 서점에다 책을 팔다
sell one's used books
to the secondhand
bookstore

온라인 서점에서
책을 구매하다
buy [order] a
book at an online
bookstore

이북(전자책)을
구매하다
buy [order]
an eBook

집으로/회사로 책을 배송받다
have books
delivered to one's
house / company

SENTENCES TO USE

미아는 자신의 책이 베스트셀러 목록에 있는지 확인하려고 서점에 들렀습니다.
Mia stopped by the bookstore to check if her book is on the bestseller list.

저기, 이 책 위치 찾는 것 좀 도와주시겠어요?
Excuse me, could you help me look for the location of this book?

저는 책을 사기 전에 항상 한 챕터를 훑어봅니다.   I always leaf through a chapter of a book before buying it.

그는 자기가 읽던 책을 절대 중고 서점에 팔지 않습니다.
He never sells his used books to the secondhand bookstore.

제이슨은 병가 중이라 집 밖을 나갈 수 없을 때 온라인으로 이북을 구입했습니다.
Jason bought eBooks online when he was on sick leave and couldn't leave his house.

MP3 033

인사를 나누다
exchange
greetings

대화를 나누다,
수다 떨다
have a chat

~의 안부를 묻다
inquire after ~

~에게 안부를 전하다
say hello to ~, send
one's regards to ~

* 주로 안부 전해 달라고
부탁할 때 쓰임.

요즘 상황을 이야기하다
talk [chat] about
current situation

화젯거리를 이야기하다
talk [chat] about the
hot topic

~을 자랑하다
brag [show off]
about [on] ~

* '~에 칭찬받다'는
get compliment on ~

~을 칭찬하다
compliment
about [on] ~

~을 후회하다
regret about [on] ~

~을 뒷말하다
talk behind one's back

작별 인사를 나누다
say goodbye [farewell]

SENTENCES TO USE

저는 매일 아침 카페 매니저와 인사를 나눕니다.
I exchange greetings with the cafe manager every morning.

요즘 화제가 되는 주제에 관해 이야기를 나누어 볼까요?
Why don't we have a chat about the current hot topic?

어머니께 대신 안부 좀 전해 주세요.　　　　　Please send my regards to your mother for me.

저는 외출할 때마다 항상 화려한 제 양산에 칭찬받아요.
I always get compliments on my colorful parasol whenever I go out.

뒷말하는 걸 좋아하지 않지만, 제 여동생이 자기 새 차 자랑할 때는 정말 싫어요.
I don't like talking behind anybody's back but I really hate it when my sister brags about her new car.

A 제이미 안녕! 잘 지내? 오랜만이다!
▶ Hello Jaime! How are you?
It's been a long time!

B 이야, 마이클 오빠.
진짜 오랜만이네.
● Hey, Michael. It's been ages!

이게 얼마 만이야?
● How long has it been?

A 네 대학교 졸업식에서 보고
처음이니 거의 2년 만이네.
▶ It's been almost 2 years
since I saw you at your college
graduation.

넌 그때나 지금이나 똑같다.
▶ You look the same now and
then.

B 오빠는 살을 많이 뺐네. 볼이
포동포동했던 사람이 이제는 아주
날씬하고 훈남이 되었어.
● And you lost a lot of weight.
The one who had a plump
face is now very slim and
handsome.

A 아이고, 무슨. 그래도 운동을 열심히
해 왔는데 달라지긴 했나 보네.
▶ Oh, please. I guess some
things have changed since I've
been working out a lot.

B 전보다 훨씬 슬림하고 멋져 보여.
● You look much slimmer and
splendid.

그동안 어떻게 지냈어?
● How are things going for
you?

A 난 이직하고 새 회사에서 자리
잡느라 일만 하고 바쁘게 살았어.
▶ I was busy settling down
in my new company after
I changed jobs.

현재 해외 영업 파트에서 일하고
있어서 많은 나라들을 오가고
있지 뭐.
▶ I'm currently working in an
overseas sales department, so
I travel to a lot of countries.

시차랑 새로운 환경에 적응하는 게
힘들긴 한데 다양한 사람들을 만나고
새로운 문화도 경험하는 게
재미있어서 잘 다니고 있지 뭐.
▶ It's hard to adjust to the
time difference and new
environment, but I'm enjoying
meeting various people and
experiencing new cultures.

너는 어떠니?
▶ How about you?

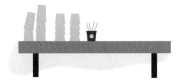

B   나는 첫 번째 회사 잘 다니다가
얼마 전에 연예 기획사 쪽으로
회사 옮겼어.
● I was doing okay at my first
company, and recently moved
to an entertainment agency.

좋은 제안을 받기도 했고 이전
직장에서 사람들 때문에
좀 힘들었거든.
● I received a good offer while
having a hard time with people
at my previous job.

A   왜, 그 회사에서 무슨 일 있었어?
거기 들어가서 일하는 게
네 로망이었잖아.
▶ Why, what happened at that
company? It was your dream to
work there.

B   회사 분위기는 너무 재밌고 좋았는데
상사 한 명이 계속 나를 못살게
굴더라고.
● The work atmosphere was
great but one of the bosses
kept tormenting me.

내가 잘못한 일도 아닌데 마치
내가 실수해서 문제가 생긴 것처럼
보고하기도 하고.
● It was not my fault, but
he reported it as if I made a
mistake and caused the issue.

얼마 전에는 내가 기획한 프로젝트
아이디어가 우수 아이디어로
채택되었는데 그 사람이
내 아이디어를 베껴서 자기 이름으로
기획서 올려 가지고는 내가 받을
상을 빼앗아 갔네.
● And not long ago, the project
idea I planned was chosen
to be the superb idea, but he
copied it and uploaded the
project under his name to take
away the award I was going to
receive.

열 받아서 바로 그만두고
지금 회사로 옮긴 거야.
● I quit and moved jobs
because I was furious.

A 와! 그거 드라마 소재감인데!
정말 짜증났겠다.
▶ Wow! That sounds like
drama material! You must have
been so frustrated.

새로 옮긴 회사는 어때?
▶ How about your new
workplace?

B 여긴 뭐 천국이지.
● This place is like heaven.

분위기도 좋고 연예인들도 많이
만나고 열심히만 하면 커리어
쌓는 데 도움이 많이 될 것 같아.
● The atmosphere is great
and I think it will help me
build a career if I meet many
celebrities and
work hard.

A 아주 좋네! 연애 사업은 어떻게
돼 가?
▶ Good to hear! How about
your love business?

B 음, 솔로로 있은 지 좀 됐지!
● Hmm, I have been single for
a while.

왜? 좋은 사람 있어?
● Why? Do you know anyone?

A 아, 사실은 있어!
▶ As a matter of fact, I do!

너 소개팅 한번 안 할래?
▶ How do you feel about a
blind date?

친한 직장 동료가 너랑 잘 어울릴 것
같아.
▶ I have a close colleague who
would get along with you.

B 소개팅? 오빠가 소개해 주는 거라면
   믿을 만한 사람일 텐데, 나야 무조건
   콜이지.

   ● A blind date? If you are
   introducing him to me, he
   should be a reliable man, so I
   am totally in!

A 오케이, 잘됐다. 그러면 내가
   일정 조율해서 자리 한번 만들어
   보고 알려 줄게.

   ▶ Okay, awesome. Then I will
   arrange the schedule and let
   you know.

CHAPTER

5

학교생활

SCHOOL LIFE

횡단보도에서 경비 아저씨에게 인사하다
greet [say hello to] the guard at the crosswalk

친구들과 문자하다
text (with) friends

사물함에 짐을 넣다
put [shove] one's stuff in one's locker

학교 운동장에서 축구를 하다
play soccer in the schoolyard

책상 정리를 하다
clean (up) one's desk

선생님께 인사하다
greet [bow to, say hello to] the teacher

SENTENCES TO USE

남자아이들 대부분이 운동장에서 축구 하는 걸 좋아합니다.
Most of the boys like to play soccer in the schoolyard.

저는 보통 수업 전에 사물함에 물건을 넣고 책상 정리를 합니다.
I usually shove my stuff in the locker and clean my desk before class.

청소 당번을 정하다
decide on clean-up duty [cleaning duty]

짝꿍을 정하다
decide on a seating partner

선생님께 혼나다
get a scolding from one's teacher,
be [get] scolded by one's teacher

수업 중에 꾸벅꾸벅 졸다
doze [nod] off
in class

공책에 낙서하다
scribble [doodle] on one's notebook

학급 게시판을 정리하다
organize one's class bulletin board

청소 당번은 매주 바뀝니다.
People on cleaning duty change every week.

학생들은 수업 중에 졸면 선생님께 혼납니다.
Students get scolded by their teacher when they doze off in class.

저는 친구와 함께 학급 게시판을 정리하곤 했습니다.
I used to organize the class bulletin board with my friend.

A 너 들었어? 우리 반 반장이 이번에 교육부 장관상을 받는대.
▶ Did you hear? Our class president is getting the Minister of Education Award.

B 우리 반 반장? 샘 말이야? 잘됐다. 뭘로 받는 건데?
● Our class president? Are you talking about Sam? Good for him. What for?

A 그치. 걔가 학교생활을 더 유익하고 의미 있게 만드는 아이디어 공모전에 나갔는데 대상을 탔대.
▶ Yes, he entered an idea contest to come up with ways to create more helpful and meaningful school life and he won the grand prize.

B 작년까지만 해도 맨날 애들이랑 싸우고 수업 땡땡이쳐서 정학받고 그랬잖아.
● Until last year, he was suspended for constantly fighting with other students and skipping classes.

어떻게 1년 사이에 달라진 거지?
● What changed in a year?

A 작년에 미인정결석 기간이 길어져서 거의 퇴학당할 뻔했는데, 우리 담임이 걔한테 마지막으로 한 번 더 열심히 해 보자고 설득하셨대.
▶ He almost got expelled last year for extended unexcused absences, but our class teacher persuaded him to give one more try.

샘에게 독서 동아리 가입을 추천해 주셨다고 하네.
▶ He recommended Sam to join the book club.

B 샘이 독서 동아리에서 엄청 열심히 활동했잖아.
● Sam worked really hard in that book club.

학교 축제에서 대박 난 독서 퀴즈 이벤트도 걔가 준비한 거라면서. 대단하다!
● I heard that he was the one who organized the book quiz event at the school event which turned out super successful. That's amazing!

A 응, 책을 많이 읽으면서 삶에 대한 태도가 확실히 달라졌다고 해.
▶ Yup, apparently his attitude toward his life has changed since he read a lot of books.

예전에는 걔가 엄마한테 수학 학원 간다고 거짓말하고 게임하러 PC방 가고 그랬잖아.
▶ He used to lie to his mom that he was going to math academy and went to an Internet cafe to play games instead.

그런데 지금은 방과 후 수업이나 학원도 안 빼먹고 스터디 카페에서 공부하고 집에 간대.
▶ But now he does not skip any after-school classes or academy, and studies at a study cafe before heading home.

B 걔가 웬일이래? 아주 철들었네.
● What happened to him? He has grown up.

A 내년에는 학생회장 선거에도 나갈 거래.
▶ I heard Sam is running for school president next year.

나도 반성하고 앞으로 더 열심히 공부해야겠어.
▶ I better reflect on myself and study harder from now on.

MP3 037

매점에 가다
go to the kiosk
[snack bar]

책상에 엎드려 낮잠 자다
lie down on
one's desk for a nap

친구와 화장실에 가다
go to the toilet with
one's friend

친구와 수다를 떨다
chat [have a chat]
with one's friend

친구와 군것질을 하다
have [eat] a snack
with one's friend

교무실에 가다
go to the teacher's
lounge

양호실에 가다
go to the nurse's office
[school infirmary]

칠판을 정리하다
clean [organize]
the board

칠판을 지우다
erase the board

* PE는 physical
education의 약자.

체육복으로 갈아입다
change into gym
[PE] clothes

쉬는 시간 종이 울리다
a recess bell rings,
a bell rings for recess

SENTENCES TO USE

톰은 쉬는 시간에 책상에 엎드려 잠깐 낮잠을 잡니다.
Tom lies down on his desk for a short nap during recess.

저는 늘 왜 여자아이들이 친구랑 화장실에 가는지 궁금했습니다.
I always wondered why girls go to the toilet with their friends.

그녀는 매점 가는 길에 친구와 수다를 떨곤 했습니다.
She used to chat with her friend on the way to the kiosk.

우리 반 반장은 쉬는 시간 종이 울리면 항상 다음 수업을 위해 칠판을 지웁니다.
Our class president always erases the board for the next class when the recess bell rings.

학생들은 체육 수업을 위해 학교 체육복으로 갈아입어야 합니다.
Students have to change into school gym clothes for PE class.

UNIT

3 수업

교과서를 펴다
open one's
textbook

공부에 집중하다
concentrate
on the study

* '귀기울여 잘 듣다'의 의미.
선생님의 수업을 듣다
listen to one's
teacher's class

선생님의 수업을 듣다
take one's
teacher's class

* '과목을 공부하다'의 의미.

손을 들고 질문하다
raise one's hand to
ask a question

선생님 질문에 대답하다
answer the teacher's
question

수업 시간에 친구와
떠들다 걸리다
get caught chatting
with one's friend in class

음악 시간에 합창을 하다
sing together in
music class

미술 시간에
그림을 그리다
paint [draw]
in art class

* experiment는 명사, 동사로 쓰임.
과학 시간에 실험을 하다
(do an) experiment in
science class

수업 시간에 멍 때리다
space out [zone out]
during class

수업을 땡땡이치다
play hooky,
skip class

시험에서 커닝하다
cheat on one's
exam [test]

SENTENCES TO USE

수업 중에 손을 들고 모든 질문에 답하는 모범생은 항상 있습니다.
There is always a model student to raise their hand in class and answer all the questions.

그는 수업 시간에 교과서에 그림을 그리다가 걸렸어요.
He got caught drawing on his textbook in class.

학교에서 따뜻한 봄바람을 맞으며 멍 때렸던 시간이 그립습니다.
I miss my time at school when I used to space out under the warm spring breeze.

제 여동생은 땡땡이를 치고 학교 밖에서 라면을 먹는 습관이 있었습니다.
My younger sister had a habit of playing hooky and eating ramen outside school.

친구가 항상 시험에서 커닝을 해서, 난 그 애를 고자질했습니다.
My friend always cheats on her test, so I told on her.

학급 회장 선거에
나가다
run for class
president

전교 회장 선거에 나가다
run for school
president

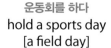

운동회를 하다
hold a sports day
[a field day]

공개 수업을 하다
have [hold]
an open class

학급 소풍을 가다
go on a class
picnic

동아리에서 탈퇴하다
withdraw
[drop out] from
a club

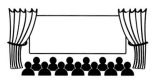

수학여행을 가다
go on a school trip
[excursion]

동아리에 가입하다
join a club
[an after-school club]

학교 축제를 준비하다
prepare for the
school festival

~에 결석하다
be absent
from ~

퇴학당하다
be [get]
expelled
from
school

조퇴하다
leave school early,
take an early leave

다른 학교로 전학 가다/
다른 학교에서 전학 오다
transfer to / from a
different school

정학을 받다
be [get] suspended
from school

SENTENCES TO USE

저는 학생 때 재미로 학급 회장 선거에 나갔습니다.　I ran for class president for fun when I was a student.

저희 부모님은 항상 제 초등학교 운동회에 오셨습니다.
My parents always came to the sports day in my elementary school.

저는 미술 동아리에 들었지만 사진 동아리에 가입하려고 그 동아리를 탈퇴했습니다.
I used to be in an art club but I dropped out from that club to join a photography club.

그는 만성 질환으로 학교를 자주 결석했습니다.
He was absent from school frequently due to chronic illness.

마이클은 수학여행에 술을 가져와서 정학을 당했습니다.
Michael got suspended from school after he brought alcohol on a school trip.

5 방과 후

MP3 040

교실을 청소하다
clean one's
classroom

친구들과 하교하다
come [return] home from
school with friends

스쿨버스를 타다
get on the
school bus

놀이터로 가다
go to the
playground

방과 후 수업을 듣다
take an
after-school class

학원 버스를 타다
take [ride] an
academy bus

OO 학원에 가다
go to academy for
OO [OO academy]

스터디 카페에 가다
go to [visit]
a study cafe

친구와
집에서 놀다
hang out with
one's friend
at home

친구집에 가다
go to [visit] one's
friend's house

게임하러 PC방에 가다
go to an Internet [a PC]
cafe to play games

숙제를 하다
do one's homework

SENTENCES TO USE

전 영어 학원 다니느라 바빠서 학교에서 친구들과 함께 하교할 기회가 전혀 없었습니다. I never had the chance to
come home from school with friends, because I was busy getting to English academy.

전 운동장에 가서 친구들과 놀려고 방과 후 수업을 땡땡이치곤 했습니다.
I used to skip the after-school class to go to the playground and play with my friends.

오늘 스쿨버스가 일찍 도착해서 샘은 친구 집에 갈 수가 없었습니다.
The school bus arrived early today, so Sam could not go to his friend's house.

엄마는 오빠(형)를 찾으러 동네 PC방에 가시곤 했습니다.
My mother used to go to a local Internet cafe to search for my older brother.

제 친구 중 한 명은 항상 스쿨버스를 타기 전에 숙제를 끝내고 가야 한다고 고집을 부렸습니다.
One of my friends always insisted on doing her homework before getting on the school bus.

MP3 **041**

학교에 출근하다
go to work
at school

조회에 참석하다
attend [go to] a
morning assembly

교실 청소 상태를 확인하다
check the cleanliness
of the classroom

교안을 준비하다
prepare [make] a teaching
plan [a lesson plan]

수업을 진행하다
conduct
one's class

학생에게 상을 주다
give an award to
a student, award
a student

문제 학생을 훈육하다
discipline a
troubled student

시험 문제를 만들다
make exam
questions

시험 감독을 하다
supervise an
examination

학생기록부를 작성하다
keep [make, write up]
a student record

학부모와 상담하다
consult one's
student's parents

문제 학생을/고민 있는
학생을 상담하다
consult [have a
consultation with] a
troubled / worried student

학생들에게 수학여행
동의서를 나누어 주다
distribute [hand out]
school excursion consent
forms to the students

SENTENCES TO USE

모든 선생님들은 매주 월요일 조회에 참석해야 합니다.
All teachers have to attend a morning assembly every Monday.

교사들이 교안을 준비하는 게 쉬운 일이 아닙니다.   Preparing a teaching plan is not an easy thing for teachers.

선생님은 수업을 진행하면서 학생들의 질문에 대답합니다.
A teacher answers the students' questions while conducting his class.

문제 학생의 부모와 학생기록부의 중요성에 관해 상담하는 건 교사 업무의 일부분입니다.
Consulting troubled student's parents about the importance of a student record is part of
teacher's job.

수학 선생님이 올해 중간고사 문제를 유난히 어렵게 내셨어요.
The math teacher made midterm exam questions especially hard this year.

대학교에 지원하다
apply for college [university]

입학 허가서를 받다
receive [get] an admission letter [a letter of admission]

등록금을 내다
pay for one's tuition

학자금 대출을 받다
take out [receive] a student loan

~을 전공하다
major in ~

수강 신청을 하다
register [sign up] for courses, enroll in classes

OT에 참여하다
participate in [experience, go through] an OT (= orientation)

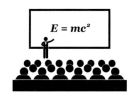

강의를 듣다
take a class

온라인 강의를 듣다
take an online class

학생회에 가입하다
join [sign up for] a student council

~을 복수 전공하다
double-major in ~

SENTENCES TO USE

저는 대학에 지원해 입학 허가서를 받게 되어 매우 기뻤습니다.
I was so excited to apply for college and get the letter of admission.

마감일까지 등록금 내는 것 잊지 마세요.
Please don't forget to pay for your tuition by the deadline.

루카스는 제시간에 수강 신청하는 것을 깜빡해서 올해 수업 시간표를 망쳤습니다.
Lucas forgot to sign up for courses on time so his class schedule is destroyed for the year.

주디는 학생회에 가입하면서 더 많은 일이 생겼습니다.
Judy added more workload by joining the student council.

그녀는 생물학과 미술사를 복수 전공하고 있습니다.
She is double-majoring in biology and art history.

장학금을 받다
get [receive]
a scholarship

학사 경고를 받다
get placed under academic
probation, receive a school warning

그룹 스터디를 하다
participate in [join]
a study group

동아리 활동을 하다
participate in [join] a
club activity

남학생 사교클럽/여학생 사교클럽에 가입하다
join a fraternity /
a sorority

그룹 과제를 하다
do a group
project

~와 도서관에서 공부하다
study in the library
with ~

~에서 혼자 공부하다
study alone at ~

~를 벼락치기하다
cram for ~,
hit the books,
last-minute study for ~

중간고사/기말고사를 치르다
take a midterm /
a final exam

SENTENCES TO USE

그녀는 학사경고를 받고 장학금을 놓쳤습니다.
She lost her scholarship after getting placed under academic probation.

그는 새 학기가 시작되었을 때 배드민턴 동아리와 스카이다이빙 동아리에 가입했습니다.
He joined a badminton club and a skydiving club when the new semester started.

대부분의 대학생들이 남녀 사교 모임 가입하는 것에 환상이 있습니다.
Most university students have a fantasy about joining a fraternity or a sorority.

저는 무임승차자 때문에 조별 과제를 하는 데 어려움을 겪었습니다.
I had issues with doing group projects because of free riders.

예전엔 중간고사를 벼락치기하곤 했는데, 지금은 그렇게 안 해요.
I used to cram for my midterms, but I don't do it anymore.

~에서 통학하다
commute from ~

기숙사 생활을 하다
live in a dormitory

자취를 하다
make one's own living, live by oneself

아르바이트를 하다
work at a part-time
job, work part-time

과외 수업을 하다
give private
lessons

캠퍼스 커플이 되다
become a college couple
[college sweethearts]

수업에 지각하다
be late
for class

휴학 신청을 하다
apply for a leave of
absence (from college)

복학 신청을 하다
apply to go back
to college

졸업 전시회를 열다
hold [have] a graduation
exhibition

SENTENCES TO USE

그녀는 수업을 들으러 도시 외곽에서 통학하고 있습니다.
She is commuting from the outskirts of the town to take classes.

새미는 군 복무하러 가기 전에 한 학기 동안 기숙사에서 살았습니다.
Sammy lived in a dormitory for one semester before going off to serve in the army.

저는 생활비를 벌기 위해 과외를 하고 아르바이트를 하기도 했습니다.
I used to give private lessons and work part-time to earn living expenses.

저는 학교에서 소개팅했던 여자와 캠퍼스 커플이 되었습니다.
I became a college couple with the girl I had a blind date with on campus.

사진 전공 졸업 전시회를 열었는데 대성공이었습니다.
We held a graduation exhibition for our photography major and it was a great success.

A 지나, 나 이번에 NIT 생명공학과에 합격했어!
▶ Gena, I got accepted to the Department of Biotechnology at NIT!

B 와! 축하해. 재수하면서 정말 열심히 공부했구나.
● Wow! Congratulations. You studied really hard to retake the entrance exam.

NIT면 네가 가고 싶어 하던 1순위 대학이잖아.
● NIT University was on the top of your list of your desired universities.

A 고마워.
▶ Thank you.

어제 OT 갔다 왔는데 교수님들도 자상해 보이고 선배들도 잘 챙겨 주고 분위기가 좋더라고.
▶ I went to the orientation yesterday, and the professors seemed kind, the senior students took good care of me and the whole atmosphere was great.

다음 주에 제임스 타운으로 MT 간다는데 정말 기대돼.
▶ I'm really looking forward to going to James Town for the get-together next week.

B 이야, 좋겠다.
● That sounds great.

이제 제대로 된 대학 생활 시작이겠구나.
● Sounds like you're starting your real college life now.

수강 신청은 너무 욕심 부리지 말고 적당히 들어.
● Take it easy and don't get greedy about registering for classes.

내가 1학년 1학기 때 24학점 신청했다가 학점 관리하느라 죽을 뻔했지 뭐야.
● I registered 24 credits for my first semester as a freshman and I almost died trying to manage my grades.

다행히 학사경고는 안 먹었지. 기말고사 두 번 말아먹고 F가 두 개나 떴거든.
● Luckily, I didn't get placed under academic probation, because I got two Fs after messing up two finals.

A 1학년 때는 동아리 활동도 열심히 해 보고 CC도 해 보고 싶어서 수업은 적당히 들어야겠네.
▶ I want to be active in club activities and experience being a college couple as a freshman, so I gotta go easy on taking classes.

1학년 마치고 미국 교환학생 지원해 1년 다녀온 다음 휴학하고 군대 갔다 와서 열심히 공부해야지.
▶ After my first year in college, I'm going to apply to be an exchange student in the U.S. for a year, take a leave of absence for military service and come back and work hard.

B 너는 앞으로의 계획을 다 잡아 놨구나! 좋겠다.
● You have all your plans for the future! Good for you.

나는 학교 자퇴하고 대학 입학 시험을 다시 볼까 고민 중이야.
● I am thinking about taking the college entrance exam again after dropping out of college.

A 왜, 무슨 일 있어?
▶ Why, what happened?

B 전공이 나랑 안 맞는 것 같아서 그래.
● I don't think my major is a good fit for me.

졸업하고 지금 전공 분야에서 잘할 수 있을지 걱정이 되네.
● I'm worried if I can do well working in this area of expertise after graduation.

A 그래? 고민이 되겠네.
▶ Really? That's a dilemma.

내 생각에는 나중에 마음 바뀔 수도 있으니까 일단 휴학해서 대학 입시 결과 보고 결정하는 게 좋을 것 같아.
▶ To give you my opinion, it would be better to take a leave of absence and decide after looking at your results for another entrance exam just in case you change your mind later on.

B 그래, 그게 최선이겠네. 고마워.
● Yeah, that seems like the best option. Thanks.

졸업 앨범 사진을 찍다
take graduation album photos

정장을 차려입다
dress oneself up

학사모를 쓰다
wear a graduation cap

졸업 가운을 입다
wear a graduation gown

졸업식에 가족을/친지를 초청하다
invite one's family /
relatives to one's graduation ceremony

졸업식에 참석하다
attend [participate in, go to] one's
graduation ceremony

SENTENCES TO USE

제 졸업식에 가족 전체가 와서 매우 기뻤습니다.
I was very happy that my whole family attended my graduation ceremony.

그녀는 가족 중에서 (대학) 졸업 가운과 학사모를 쓴 첫 번째 사람이었습니다.
She was the first one to wear a graduation gown and cap in her family.

졸업장을 받다
get [receive] a diploma

학사모를 던지다
throw one's graduation cap

동기들과 졸업 사진을 찍다
take graduation
photos with
one's classmates

졸업생 대표의 연설을 듣다
listen to the
valedictorian speech

학장님/총장님의 축사를 듣다
listen to the dean's / president's
congratulatory speech

우리는 이 졸업장을 따기 위해 정말 열심히 공부했습니다!
We worked so hard to get this diploma!

모두가 학사모를 공중에 던지는 사진을 찍습니다.
Everyone takes a photo of throwing their graduation cap in the air.

학장님의 축사를 듣는 게 지루했습니다.
Listening to the dean's congratulatory speech was a drag.

6

직장 생활

LIFE AT WORK

구직 활동

일자리를 찾다
look [search] for a job (position),
seek employment

이력서/지원서를 쓰다
write a resume
/ an application

자기소개서를 쓰다
write a self-introduction letter
[a cover letter]

직무 적성 검사를 하다
conduct [get] a job aptitude
test

교수님에게 추천서를 부탁드리다
ask the professor for a letter of
recommendation [reference, referral]

SENTENCES TO USE

제 친구들과 저는 인턴으로 일자리를 찾기 시작했습니다.
My friends and I started looking for jobs as an intern.

지원서와 자기소개서를 수없이 많은 회사에 보냈지만, 아무도 제게 연락을 주지 않았습니다.
I sent tons of applications and cover letters to multiple companies, but none called me back.

소피아는 직무 적성 검사를 받았고 회사가 자신에게 맞지 않는다는 것을 바로 알았습니다.
Sophia got a job aptitude test and she knew right away that the company was not a good fit
for her.

저는 서로 다른 교수님 세 분께 받은 추천서가 세 장 필요합니다.
I need three letters of recommendation from three different professors.

회사에 지원하다
apply to a company

면접을 기다리다
wait for a job interview

면접을 보다
have [go to] an
interview

합격/불합격 통보를 받다
receive [get] a notification [letter] of
acceptance / rejection

대기자 통보를 받다
receive a waiting notice,
get wait-listed

면접을 기다리면서 굉장히 마음이 초조했습니다.
I was very nervous waiting for a job interview.

취업 대기자 명단에 오르는 건 좋은 기분이 아닙니다.
It's not a good feeling to get wait-listed for a job position.

A 우리 회사에 지원해 주셔서
감사합니다.
▶ Thank you for applying to
our company.

이력서와 자기소개서 잘 봤고요.
▶ We have gone through your
resume and cover letter.

현장 실습 경험도 풍부하고 학교
다니면서 다양한 대외활동을
하셨더군요.
▶ You seem to have a lot of
experience in field training,
as well as various outside
activities while attending
school.

B 네, 대학교 총학생회장을 하면서
학과와 관련된 행정 일을 많이
경험했습니다.
● Yes, I experienced a lot of
administrative work related
to the department while I was
student body president of the
university.

제 담당 교수님 밑에서 다양한
프로젝트를 진행하면서 기업
관계자분들과 원활히 소통하려고
노력했습니다.
● And I worked hard for
smooth communication
with corporate officials while
working on various projects
under my professor.

A 직무 적성 검사 결과도 매우
우수하군요.
▶ The job aptitude test also
showed very good results.

다만 한 가지 궁금한 게 이전
회사에서 짧게 5개월 근무하고
퇴사했는데 혹시 퇴사한 이유를
말씀해 주실 수 있나요?
▶ One thing we are curious
about is that you left your
previous workplace after
working for a short 5 month.
Could you tell us the reason?

B 전 회사의 분위기와 동료분들은
너무 좋았는데 제가 맡은 직무가
제가 가장 잘할 수 있는 일이
아니었습니다.
● The atmosphere of the
previous office and colleagues
were great, but my job
description was not something
I could do best.

제 능력을 최대한 발휘할 수 있는 직무에서 일하는 것이 회사에도 도움이 되고 저에게도 동기 부여가 되는 것 같아서 너무 늦기 전에 빠르게 이직을 결정했습니다.

● I decided to move on to a different job quickly before it was too late, because working in a position where I perform best with my abilities to the fullest might help this company and motivate me.

A 아, 네 그러셨군요. 입사하게 되면 어떤 일을 해 보고 싶은가요?

▶ Oh, yes, I see. What do you plan to do if you join our company?

B 제가 학교에서 다양한 일들을 해 보고 그런 프로젝트에서 많은 기업 관계자를 만나 보면서 제가 대인관계를 잘 관리하고 소통 능력이 우수하다는 것을 알게 되었습니다.

● As I participated in various activities in college and met many company representatives in such projects, I learned that I am good at managing interpersonal relationships and have excellent communication skills.

귀사에 입사한다면 제 이러한 능력을 최대한 발휘할 수 있게 영업 지원팀에서 일하고 싶습니다.

● If I get the chance to join your company, I would like to work in the sales support team so that I can show my abilities to the fullest.

A 답변 감사합니다.

▶ Thank you for your answer.

이번 주까지 면접을 마치고 다음주에 결과 통보 드리겠습니다. 수고 많으셨습니다.

▶ We will finish up the interview by this week and let you know the result next week. Thank you for your effort.

| 회사에 들어가다
join [enter] a
company [a firm] | 출근하다
go to work
[the office], report
for duty | 하루 일정을 확인하다
check the schedule for
the day, check one's
daily schedule | 인턴을 하다
do an internship,
become an intern |

| 신입사원 교육을 받다
receive [get]
training for new
employees | 현장 실습을 하다
conduct field
training | 상사의 업무 지시를 듣다
listen to [follow] one's
boss's instructions | 상사에게 업무
보고를 하다
report to
one's boss | 메모를 하다
take notes
[a memo] |

| 초과 근무 수당을 받다
get overtime pay,
get paid overtime | 사원증을 재발급받다
get an employee card
[badge] reissued | 회사 메신저로 메시지를 보내다
send a message through
the company messenger |

SENTENCES TO USE

올리버는 회사에 들어가서 신입사원 교육 시작을 고대하고 있습니다.　　Oliver is looking forward to entering a company and starting his training as a new employee.

그는 상사와 하루 일정을 확인하는 습관이 있습니다.
He has a habit of checking his daily schedule with his supervisor.

윌리엄은 스케줄을 확인하고 상사의 지시를 따르는 데 매우 엄격합니다.
William is very strict on checking schedules and following his supervisor's instructions.

크리스 씨께 전할 메시지가 있다면 제가 메모해 놓겠습니다.
I can take a memo if you have a message for Mr. Chris.

한번은 홀리가 회사 메신저를 통해 당혹스러운 사적인 메시지를 보낸 적이 있습니다.
Holly once sent an embarrassing private message through the company messenger.

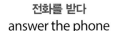

전화를 받다
answer the phone

전화를 돌려주다
transfer a phone call

전화를 끊다
hang up the phone

자료/서류를 정리하다
organize one's
material / file

서류 작업을 하다
complete [write up]
a document (file),
do paperwork

~을 복사하다
make some
copies of ~

서류에 도장을 찍다
stamp the
document

서류를 제출하다
submit the
document

상사에게 결재를 받다
obtain [get] approval from the boss,
get a sanction from the boss

서류를 팩스/이메일로 보내다
send a document
by fax / e-mail

서류를 파기하다
shred a
document

SENTENCES TO USE

누군가가 전화로 얘기 중인데 전화를 끊는 건 실례입니다.
It is rude to hang up the phone when someone is talking on the line.

통제 불능이 되기 전에 파일을 정리하도록 하세요.
Please organize your files before things get out of hand.

저 회사 그만뒀어요. 제가 한 일이라고는 서류 복사와 도장 찍는 것뿐이었거든요.
I quit my job because all I did was making copies of documents and stamping them.

그 팩스 보내기 전에 상사 결재 받는 것 잊지 마세요.
Don't forget to get approval from the boss before you send the fax.

신입사원일 때 제가 실수로 중요한 서류를 파기한 적이 있습니다.
When I was a new employee, I accidentally shredded important documents.

발표를 준비하다
prepare for one's presentation

회의실을 예약하다
book a room for a meeting

Time for a meeting.

회의 참가자들에게 참석을 요청하다
ask the conference participants to attend

PLAN

(아침) 회의에 참석하다
attend a (morning) meeting

자료를 준비하고 복사물을 나눠 주다
prepare one's material and
distribute copies

SENTENCES TO USE

올리비아가 처음 발표 준비를 하는 거라서 그녀는 매우 긴장했습니다.
It was Olivia's first time to prepare for a presentation and she was very nervous.

저는 회의실 예약하는 것을 깜빡해서 상사에게 혼났습니다.
I was scolded by my boss for forgetting to reserve a meeting room.

막내 팀원이 회의 전에 서류를 복사하고 나눠 줍니다.
The youngest co-worker makes copies and distributes the documents before the meeting.

회의에서 발언하다
speak at a meeting

팀원들과 회의를 하다
have a meeting with the team

반대 의견을 내다
have [show, take]
an opposite opinion [view]

해외 고객들과 화상회의를 하다
hold a videoconference
with overseas clients [customers]

서로의 의견을 취합하다
collect [gather] each
other's opinions

향후 전략을 제시하다/논의하다
come up with / discuss future strategies

회의를 끝내다
end the meeting

시차 때문에 해외 고객들과 화상 회의를 하는 게 쉽지 않습니다.
Due to the time difference, it is not easy to hold a videoconference with overseas customers.

우리 의견을 취합해서 향후 전략을 짜내 봅시다.
Let's gather our opinions and come up with a future strategy.

A 회의 준비 다 됐습니다.
▶ We are good to go with the meeting.

B 네, 오늘 회의는 어제 크리스 씨가 참석한 미팅에 대한 성과 보고예요.
● Okay, today's meeting is about an outcome report of the meeting Mr. Chris attended yesterday.

크리스 씨, 발표 진행하세요.
● Please proceed with the presentation, Mr. Chris.

A 감사합니다. 어제 XYZ사 전략 기획 팀에 저희 서비스를 소개하고 시연 했는데 반응이 꽤 좋았습니다.
▶ Thank you very much. Yesterday, we introduced our service to XYZ's strategic planning team and demonstrated it, and the response was very good.

그쪽에서 제품의 세부 스펙도 꼼꼼히 확인하고 기술 관련된 질문도 많이 하셨어요.
▶ They carefully checked the specifications of the product and asked a lot of questions about the technology as well.

미팅 끝나고 점심 식사도 같이했는데 저희 제품에 대한 칭찬을 계속해 주더라고요.
▶ We had lunch together afterwards, and they kept complimenting us on our products.

B 오, 술술 잘 풀리는 것 같은데요.
● Oh, it seems like everything is going well.

크리스 씨가 보기에는 어떻게 될 것 같아요?
● Mr. Chris, how do you think things will proceed?

A 일단 그쪽 팀장님이 회사 대표님께 보고하기 전에 기술 관련한 엔지니어 미팅을 요청하셨습니다.
▶ First, their team leader requested an engineer meeting regarding the technology before reporting to their CEO.

개발자들끼리 기술 이전 관련 회의를 진행한 다음에 보고를 할 것 같아요.
▶ It seems like their developers will report after conducting a meeting on technology transfer.

B 그렇군요. 기술과 관련된 세부
내용은 우리 회사 특허 기술도 있고
기밀 정보가 많으니 기밀 유지 협약
(NDA)을 먼저 맺은 다음에
회의를 진행해야 해요.
● I see. Details related to
the technology include our
patented technology and a lot
of confidential information, so
we need them to sign the NDA
(Non-Disclosure Agreement)
first and then proceed with
the meeting.

A 네. 이미 그쪽 팀장님께 기밀 유지
협약서에 관해 이메일을 보냈고
미팅 전에 체결하기로 했습니다.
▶ Yes, ma'am. I've already
emailed their team leader
about the confidentiality
agreement and decided to
sign it before the meeting.

엔지니어 회의가 잘 되면
그다음에는 어떻게 할까요?
▶ If the engineer meeting
goes well, how should we
proceed to the next step?

B 그다음에는 우리 대표님에게
보고를 드리고 공식적인 MOU
(업무 협약) 제안서를 준비하세요.
● After that, report to our
representatives and prepare
an official MOU proposal.

상대편에서 MOU에 동의하면
미팅을 해 양사 대표님이 MOU
체결을 하게 하고 이 내용을
언론사에 보도자료로 배포하세요.
● If the other party agrees
to the MOU, have another
meeting for both CEOs to sign
the MOU and distribute the
contents for press release.

A 네, 알겠습니다. 세부적인 협상은
MOU가 체결된 뒤에
진행되겠군요.
▶ Yes, ma'am. I guess the
detailed negotiations will
proceed after the MOU is
signed.

말씀하신 순서대로
진행하겠습니다.
▶ I will proceed in the order
you said.

MP3 051

거래처와 협의하다
consult a client

SURVEY

고객 만족도 조사를 하다
conduct a customer
satisfaction survey

THANK YOU

고객에게 감사 메시지를 보내다
send a thank you message
to the customer

거래처를[고객을] 만나다
meet a client

고객과 명함을 주고받다
exchange business
cards with a client

blah blah

고객[거래처]에게
설명하다
explain to the client

고객[거래처]의 질문에 답하다
answer the client's
questions

고객과 커피를 마시다
have [drink] a coffee
with one's client

고객과[거래처와] 계약을 체결하다
sign a contract with
the client

고객의 소비 패턴을 분석하다
analyze customer
consumption patterns

SENTENCES TO USE

주요 기업들은 매년 고객 만족도 조사를 실시하고 고객을 이해하려고 합니다. Major companies conduct an annual customer satisfaction survey and try to understand customers.

보통 회의하기 전에 명함을 주고받는데, 명함이 다 떨어졌습니다.
We usually exchange business cards before meetings, but we ran out.

우리 팀은 계약 체결 전에 고객에게 매출 감소에 관해 설명해야 했습니다.
My team had to explain to the client about our decrease in sales before signing a contract.

저는 사무실에서 상담 후 고객과 커피를 마셨습니다.
I had a coffee with my client after our consultation in the office.

제품을 만들기 전에 고객의 소비 패턴을 반드시 분석하도록 하세요.
Make sure to analyze customer consumption patterns before making the products.

5 외부 활동

외근을 가다
work outside
of the office

출장을 가다
go on a
business trip

거래처를 돌아다니며 영업을 하다
go around doing
business

견적서를 이메일로 보내다
e-mail
an estimate

**주문 수량에 따른
가격 차이를 설명하다**
explain the price
difference in order
quantities

영수증을 경리부에 전달하다
pass one's receipt on to the
accounting department

경비를 환급받다
get reimbursed for
one's expenses

제품을 포장하다
package the
product

운송장을 발행하다
issue an invoice
[a waybill]

~을 택배로 발송하다
deliver ~ by [send ~
through] courier

경쟁사 제품과 장단점을 비교하다
compare pros and cons
with competitor's products

SENTENCES TO USE

샐리는 홍콩으로 일주일간 출장을 가게 되어 신났습니다.
Sally was excited to go on a one-week business trip to Hong Kong.

회의 전에 고객에게 견적서를 이메일로 보내기로 했는데 제가 깜빡했습니다.
I was supposed to email an estimate to the client before the meeting, but I forgot.

경리부에 영수증 전달하지 않으면, 경비 환급이 안 됩니다.
Unless you pass the receipt on to the accounting department, you won't get reimbursed.

제품을 포장해서 택배로 발송하는 직원이 따로 있습니다.
There is an employee who packages the product and sends it through courier.

그는 경쟁사 제품과 장단점을 비교하고 그 보고서를 팩스로 보냈습니다.
He compared pros and cons with the competitor's products and sent the report by fax.

6 점심시간

12:30 PM

구내식당에서 (밥을) 먹다
eat in the cafeteria

점심시간을 갖다
take a lunch break

누구와 점심 먹을지 생각하다
think about who to have lunch with

무엇을 먹을지 정하다
decide what to eat

점심을 거르다
skip lunch

도시락을 먹다
eat a box(ed) lunch

SENTENCES TO USE

상사와 같이 점심 먹을 생각을 하니 체할 것 같습니다.
I'm afraid the thought of having lunch with my boss gives me an upset stomach.

항상 점심으로 무엇을 먹을지 생각하죠.
I always think about what to eat for lunch.

에바는 점심을 거르고 점심시간에 필라테스 수업을 받기 시작했습니다.
Ava started skipping lunch and taking Pilates lessons during lunch hours.

회사 주변 식당에 가다
go to [visit] a restaurant near one's company

점심시간에 자기 개발을 하다
self-develop during lunch hours

낮잠을 자다
take a nap

회사 주변을 산책하다
take a walk around the company

식사 후 커피 타임을 가지다
take a coffee break after lunch

우리는 점심 먹으러 회사 근처 작은 지역 음식점에 가는 것을 좋아합니다.
We like to visit small local food restaurants near our company for lunch.

몇몇 직원들은 점심 식사 후에 낮잠을 자거나 커피를 마시며 휴식을 취합니다.
Several employees either take a nap or take a coffee break after lunch.

보너스를 받다
get [receive]
a bonus

신입사원을 모집하다
recruit new employees
[workers]

Good job...

회사에 성과 보고를 하다
report achievements
to the company

(~에서) 퇴사하다
resign (from)

You are promoted.

(성과를 인정받아) 승진하다
be [get] promoted (in recognition of one's achievements)

연봉을 협상하다
negotiate for one's salary

(~에서) 은퇴하다
retire (from)

SENTENCES TO USE

클로이는 성과를 인정받아 보너스를 받고 승진했습니다.
Chloe was promoted in recognition of her achievements along with a bonus.

그녀는 은퇴하기 전에 연봉을 협상할 기회가 없었습니다.
She never got the chance to negotiate for her salary before she retired.

해고당하다
be [get] fired [dismissed]

사직서를 내다
hand in one's resignation

이직하다
change one's job,
move to a different company

회사 법무팀의 감사를 받다
get audited by the
company's legal team

(징계 조치로) 정직 처분을 받다
receive suspension
(as a disciplinary measure)

감봉 처분을 받다
get a pay cut [a disposition
of salary reduction]

회사 징계위원회에 회부되다
be sent [referred, submitted]
to the corporate disciplinary
committee

저는 전 직장에서 부당하게 해고되었고 아직 재판이 끝나지 않았습니다.
I was wrongfully dismissed from my previous workplace and the trials are not over yet.

감봉되느니 차라리 다른 회사로 옮기겠어요.
I'd rather move to a different company than get a pay cut.

A 지난해 실적이 아주 우수하군요. 입사한 지 2년 만에 조기 승진한 것 축하합니다.

▶ Your performance last year was very good. Congratulations on your early promotion in 2 years.

B 감사합니다. 좋은 팀원들과 함께 일할 수 있어서 성과가 잘 나온 것 같습니다.

● I appreciate that. I believe the results came out as such because I was able to work with good team members.

A 겸손하시네요! 초과 근무 시간과 영업 실적을 보면 그 팀이 얼마나 열심히 했는지가 보이는데요.

▶ How modest! I can see how hard your team worked through the overtime hours and sales performances.

작년 성과에 대한 보너스는 회사 규정에 따라 다음 분기 말에 개별 지급될 겁니다.

▶ Bonus for last year's performance will be paid separately at the end of next quarter in accordance with the company's regulations.

B 감사합니다. 이전 회사에서 이직하면서 내가 이 일을 잘해 낼 수 있을까 걱정했는데 저에게 딱 맞는 일을 하게 되어 회사 생활이 즐겁습니다.

● Thank you so much. I was worried about whether I could do this job well when I moved from my previous company, but now I am enjoying my work life with a job that suits me.

A 네, 저희도 하버스 씨 같은 분과 함께 일해서 기쁩니다. 본론으로 들어가서, 내년 임금에 대해서 어느 정도의 인상을 기대하시나요?

▶ Yes, we are also happy to be working with someone like you, Mr. Harbers. To get to the point, how much increase do you expect in next year's salary?

B 작년에 제가 보여드린 성과도 있고 이번에 큰 프로젝트도 최근에 수주한 것이 있으니 괜찮으시다면 기존 연봉의 30% 인상을 요청하고 싶습니다.

● Since I showed you the result of last year's performance and recently landed a big contract for a project this time, if you don't mind, I'd like to ask for a 30% increase from my current salary.

A 30% 인상이요? 저희가 생각하고 있던 것보다 높은 편이긴 합니다. 하지만 작년에 실적이 매우 좋았던 것은 사실이니 긍정적으로 검토해 보겠습니다. 그 밖에 요구사항이 있으신가요?

▶ 30% increase? It's higher than what we were thinking. However, it is true that last year's performance was very good, so we will review it positively. Do you have any other requirements?

B 네, 휴가일 수는 전년보다 5일 더 주시면 좋겠어요. 프로젝트 수주에 대한 보너스는 (지금보다) 20% 더 인상해 주시면 좋겠습니다.

● Yes, I'd like 5 more days of vacation added on to my previous year. Also, I would appreciate it if you could raise the bonus for the project contracts by 20% more.

A 네, 휴가일 수는 그렇게 해드릴 수 있을 것 같은데 보너스 인상은 저희에게도 부담입니다. 그러면 휴가일 수 5일 추가에 연봉 25% 인상, 보너스 10% 인상으로 제안 드리려 하는데 어떠신가요?

▶ Yes, I think we can do that for the vacation days, but the bonus increase could be a burden for us. We would like to suggest an additional 5 days of vacation days, a 25% salary increase, and a 10% bonus increase. What do you think?

B 음… 며칠 고민해 보고 말씀드려도 될까요? 사실 지금보다 더 좋은 조건으로 이직 제의를 받아서 제가 생각한 최소한의 인상 폭으로 제안을 드린 것인데 협의가 안 되는 것 같아서 생각해 볼 시간이 필요합니다.

● Hmm… Can I think about it for a few days and get back to you? In fact, I was offered a job change under better conditions, so I suggested a minimum increase. Since the negotiation didn't go through as I thought it would, I need some time to think.

A 문제없습니다. 고민해 보시고 다음 주 수요일에 뵙고 어떻게 정하셨는지 알려 주시죠. 수고하셨어요.

▶ No problem. Please think about it and let us meet next Wednesday to tell us your decision. Thank you for your efforts.

업무일지를 작성하다
keep [draw up] a daily work log

초과 근무하다
work after hours [overtime]

책상 위를 정리하다
organize the top of one's desk

* clock in은 출근,
clock out은
퇴근할 때 찍음.

출퇴근 기록기에 카드를 찍다
clock in, clock out

퇴근 후 친구를 만나다
meet up with a friend after work

워라밸을 누리다
have work-life balance

SENTENCES TO USE

저는 퇴근 전에 업무일지 작성하는 걸 거의 잊지 않습니다.
I rarely forget to draw up my daily work log before I get off work.

제이미는 매달 말이면 초과 근무하는 것에 지쳤어요.
Jaime is tired of working overtime at the end of every month.

정시 퇴근을 하면, 우리는 아마도 완벽한 워라밸을 누리겠지요.
We probably will have perfect work-life balance if we leave work on the dot.

퇴근 후 운동하러 가다
go workout [exercise] after work

악기 연주를 배우다
learn to play an instrument

동료와 모여 저녁 식사를 하다
get together for dinner with one's co-worker

동료와 술을 마시다
have a drink with one's co-worker

노래방에 가다
go to karaoke

05:00 PM

정시 퇴근(칼퇴)하다
leave work on the dot

퇴근 후 동료와 술 마시는 것은 괜찮지만, 상사와 마시는 것은 절대 안 괜찮아요.
It's okay to have a drink with my co-worker after work, but never with my boss.

우리 팀은 볼링을 치러 가거나 노래방에 갑니다.
Our team usually goes bowling or goes to karaoke.

병원

HOSPITAL

MP3 057

*미국 병원에서는
의료보험증을 보여줌.

동네 의원/(종합)병원에 들르다
stop by a local
clinic / a hospital

의료보험증을 보여주다
show one's medical
insurance card

초진을 받다
receive one's
first medical
examination

간호사가 부를 때까지
대기하다
wait for a nurse
to call

진료를 예약하다
make an appointment
with the doctor
[a doctor's appointment]

의사 소견서를
종합병원에 제출하다
submit [give] a doctor's
note to a general hospital

처방전을 받다
receive [get]
a prescription

진료비를 결제하다
settle [pay for] the
medical expenses

진료비 영수증을 받다
receive [get] a
receipt for medical
expenses

진단서를 발급하다
issue a medical
certificate [a
written diagnosis]

보험회사에 진료비를 청구하다
charge an insurance
company for
medical expenses,
claim on the insurance

입원 수속을 밟다
go through procedures
for hospitalization [the
hospitalization process]

SENTENCES TO USE

간호사나 의사가 부를 때까지 가만히 앉아서 기다려 주세요.
Please sit still and wait until a nurse or a doctor calls on you.

여기는 예약 없이는 이용 못하는 진료소라 오시기 전에 진료 예약을 하셔야 합니다.   You need to make a doctor's
appointment before you come because this is not a walk-in clinic.

이 동네 의원은 의료 자원이 한정되어 있어서, 이 의사 소견서를 종합병원에 가져가셔야 합니다.
This local clinic has limited resources so you must take this doctor's note to a general hospital.

진료비 영수증 받고 처방전 받으러 갑시다.
Let's go get the prescription after we get the receipt for our medical expenses.

저 지금 바로 입원 수속을 밟아야 합니다.
I need to go through the hospitalization process right now.

2 진료

MP3 058

진료실로 들어가다
go [walk] into the
doctor's office

진료를 받다
receive [get] medical
treatment [care]

How are you feeling?

(의사가) 환자의 건강 상태를 묻다
ask about health state of a patient,
inquire about a patient's health

청진기로 검진하다
examine [check]
with a stethoscope

맥박을 재다(확인하다)
take [check for]
a pulse

체온을 재다
take one's
temperature

MRI를 찍다
take
an MRI

* 'X-ray 사진을 찍다'는
take an X-ray

엑스레이 찍은 걸 살펴보다
take a look at
an X-ray

의사 소견서를 작성하다
write [make] a doctor's note

진료 결과를 환자에게 설명하다
explain the results of the
treatment to the patient

다른 전문의와 협진하다
cooperate with other
specialists

SENTENCES TO USE

진료를 받고 싶으시면, 건강 상태에 대해 정직하게 말씀해 주세요.
If you want to receive medical care, be honest about your health state.

간호사, 교통사고 피해자 맥박 좀 확인해 주겠어요?
Nurse, could you check for a pulse on the car accident victim?

진료실 들어가기 전에 체온을 재 봅시다.
Let's take your temperature before you walk into the doctor's office.

환자분 팔이 부러지지 않았는지 엑스레이 찍은 걸 확인해 봐야겠어요.
We need to take a look at your X-ray to make sure your arm is not broken.

진료 결과를 환자에게 설명해야 하는 의사의 입장을 생각해 보셨나요? Have you considered the doctor's
situation to explain the results of the treatment to the patient?

A   어디가 불편하세요?
▶ What seems to be the problem?

B   며칠째 왼쪽 아랫배가 살살 아파요.
● I've had a slight pain in my lower left stomach for a few days.

속이 메스껍고 답답하기도 하고 가끔 아랫배를 바늘로 찌르는 것처럼 통증이 오네요.
● I feel nauseous and stuffy, and I feel stabbing pain in my lower abdomen from time to time.

A   소화기관 쪽에 만성질환이 있으세요?
▶ Do you have any chronic diseases in your digestive system?

B   음, 작년에 급성 장염을 한 번 앓은 적은 있는데 제가 아는 한 만성질환은 없어요.
● Well, I had acute enteritis once last year, but as far as I know, I don't have a chronic disease.

A   최근에 내시경이나 초음파 검사 받으신 적 있나요?
▶ Have you had an endoscopy or ultrasound recently?

B   2개월 전에 건강검진 받을 때 위와 대장 내시경을 받았는데, 용종 몇 개 제거한 것 말고는 큰 문제 없었어요.
● I had a gastro fiberscope and a colonoscopy when I had a medical check-up two months ago, but there was no big problem other than having a few polyps removed.

A   알겠습니다. 최근에 과음을 하거나 과식을 하거나 아니면 날것을 드신 적이 있나요?
▶ Okay. Have you been overdrinking, overeating, or have eaten raw food recently?

B 지난주에 바닷가에 가서 해삼하고 소라 회를 먹었어요.
● I went to the beach last week and ate sea cucumber and conch sashimi.

그 뒤로 속이 불편한 것 같기도 하네요.
● I guess I feel uncomfortable after that.

A 배변은 어떠세요?
▶ How's your bowel movement?

B 원래 변비가 심했는데 이번 주 부터는 설사를 시작하더라고요.
● I used to have severe constipation, but I started having diarrhea this week.

A 그렇군요. 식중독일 수도 있으니 일단 약 처방해 드릴 테니까, 약 복용 후에도 속이 계속 불편하시면 오셔서 정밀 검사를 받아 보시죠.
▶ I see. It is most likely food poisoning, so I will prescribe you some medicine and you can come back for a thorough examination if you feel uncomfortable even after taking it.

B 네, 선생님, 감사합니다. 이거 보험 처리 되는 거죠?
● Okay, thank you doctor. Is this covered by insurance?

A 밖의 원무과 직원에게 말씀하시면 자세히 안내해 드릴 거예요.
▶ Have a talk with the administration staff outside and they will guide you in detail.

건강 관련 설문지를 작성하다
fill out [write in] a health survey

종합 건강 검진을 받다
get a full body check-up [a medical check-up]

키를 재다
take [measure] one's height

몸무게를 재다
take [measure] one's weight

혈압을 재다
take [measure] one's blood pressure

심박수를 확인하다
check one's heart rate

SENTENCES TO USE

의사를 만나기 전에 건강 설문지를 작성해야 합니다.
You have to fill out this health survey before meeting the doctor.

건강 검진을 받을 때 간호사가 제 키와 몸무게를 쟀습니다.
The nurse measured my height and weight when I was getting a medical check-up.

어지러우시면 저희가 혈압을 재 보면 어떨까요?
If you feel dizzy, why don't we take your blood pressure?

혈액 검사를 하다
take [do] a blood test

대변/소변 검사를 하다
have one's bowels / urine tested,
make [have] a stool test

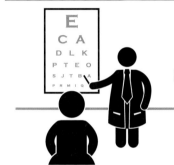

시력 검사를 하다
have one's
eyes examined
[tested, checked],
get an eye exam

청력 검사를 하다
have one's hearing examined [tested,
checked], get an audiometry

(~에) 초음파 검사를 받다
get [have] an
ultrasound (on ~)

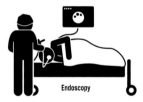

내시경 검사를 받다
have [undergo] an endoscopy
[an endoscope procedure]

그는 혈액 검사를 받아서 감염된 건지를 알아내야 합니다.
He needs to take a blood test and find out whether he is infected.

저 갑상선 초음파 검사 받으러 병원에 갈 거예요.
I am going to the hospital to get an ultrasound on my thyroid.

의사 & 간호사

팔에 주사를 놓다
give an injection [a shot]
in one's arm

팔에 수액을 맞다
get an IV (intravenous) in one's arm,
be put on an IV (intravenous)

응급처치를 하다
give first aid, take emergency
measures, seek emergency care

처방을 내리다
prescribe

환자 차트를 정리하다
organize a patient chart

SENTENCES TO USE

저는 도움이 필요한 사람들에게 응급처치하는 법을 배웠습니다.
I learned how to give first aid to those in need.

그 약은 보통 위궤양에 처방됩니다.
The drug is usually prescribed for a gastric ulcer.

회진을 돌다
do [make] one's rounds

운동 처방을 하다
prescribe exercise, present [give]
prescription of exercise

~ 수술을 받다
go through [undergo] a ~ surgery

~ 수술을 하다
perform a ~ surgery, operate on ~

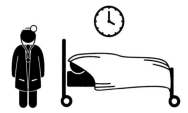

사망 선고를 받다
be pronounced dead

사망 선고를 내리다
pronounce one's death

부검을 하다
do [perform] an autopsy

의사는 환자가 허리 수술에서 회복된 후에 운동 처방을 했습니다.
The doctor prescribed exercise after the patient recovered from his back surgery.

노아는 어렸을 때 심장 수술을 받았습니다.
Noah went through a heart surgery when he was a child.

안타깝게도, 그는 병원에 도착하기도 전에 사망 선고를 받았습니다.
Unfortunately, he was pronounced dead before he could get to the hospital.

환자가 갑자기 사망한 이유를 알아내기 위해 부검을 해야 합니다.
We need to do an autopsy to find out the reason why the patient suddenly became deceased.

~가 아프다
have a(n) ~ ache, feel [have]
a pain in one's ~

머리가 지끈지끈하다
have a throbbing
headache

편두통이 있다
have a migraine

몸살 기운이 있다
have a
body ache

감기에 걸리다
catch a cold

~가 욱신욱신하다
have [feel] a throbbing
ache [pain] in one's ~

~가 저리다
have [feel] a
numbness in one's ~,
feel ~ is asleep

~가 불편하다
feel uncomfortable
in one's ~

~에 화상을 입다, ~를 데이다
get a burn on ~,
burn one's ~

~에 경련이 일어나다
have a spasm
[a cramp] in ~

~에 걸리다
come down
with the ~

SENTENCES TO USE

운동 후에 전 근육통이 심해요.
I have an intense muscle ache after my workout session.

집에서 뛰어다니지 좀 마. 머리가 지끈거린다.
Please don't run around in the house, I have a throbbing headache.

그는 몇 시간 동안 앉아 있었더니 다리가 저렸습니다.
He had a numbness in his legs after sitting down for hours.

저는 어렸을 때 끓는 물을 쏟아서 손가락을 데었어요.
I burned my fingers by spilling boiling water when I was little.

아멜리아는 비에 흠뻑 젖은 뒤 독감에 걸렸어요.
Amelia came down with the flu after she got wet in the rain.

식은땀이 나다, 식은땀을 흘리다
break out in a cold sweat, have night sweats

기침이 나다, 기침을 하다
cough, have a cough

가래가 끓다
have phlegm, have a frog in one's throat

배탈이 나다
have an upset stomach [a stomachache], suffer from indigestion

속이 울렁거리다, 메슥거리다
feel [get] nausea [sick, queasy], feel nauseous

어지럽다
feel dizzy [light-headed]

열이 나다
run [have] a fever

황달기가 있다
have jaundice

가렵다, 근질근질하다
have [get] an itch

호흡 곤란을 겪다
have difficulty breathing

코피가 나다
have [get] a bloody nose [a nosebleed]

~에 알레르기 반응을 보이다
have an allergic reaction to ~

SENTENCES TO USE

주말 내내 식은땀이 나고 몸살 기운이 있었어요.
I had night sweats and body aches throughout the weekend.

그는 일주일 내내 기침을 했습니다.
He has had a cough all week.

정신을 잃기 전에 전 속이 좀 메스꺼웠어요.
I was feeling a little queasy before I passed out.

그 사람 얼굴 봤어요? 확실히 황달기가 있어요!
Did you see his face? He definitely has jaundice!

제 아들은 알레르기 반응이 있을 때마다 가려워합니다.
My son gets an itch whenever he has an allergic reaction.

~를 꿰매다/~를 봉합하다
stitch up ~ /
suture ~

종양을 제거하다
excise [remove]
a tumor

개복 수술을 받다
get [undergo]
a laparotomy

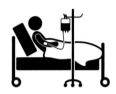

수혈을 받다
get [receive] a blood
transfusion

조직 검사를 하다
take [do]
a biopsy

* ~잘려 나간 걸 다시
붙이는 것을 의미.

~를 접합하다
join [connect] ~

~를 이식하다
transplant ~,
have a ~ transplant

물리 치료를 하다
carry out [get, do]
physical therapy

약물 치료를 하다
take medication,
be treated with
medication [drugs]

재활/수술 경과를 확인하다
check the progress of
rehabilitation /
the operation [surgery]

수술 경과가 양호하다(좋다)
progress after surgery
is good, postoperative
recovery has been good

SENTENCES TO USE

엄마는 부엌에서 손가락을 베인 후 손가락을 꿰매야 했습니다.
My mom had to get her finger stitched up after she cut her finger in the kitchen.

간 생검을 통해 양성인지 악성인지 확인해야 합니다.
We need to do a liver biopsy to determine if it's benign or malignant.

그는 그 사고 후에 물리 치료를 계속해야 했습니다.
He had to continue with physical therapy after the accident.

다음 주에 재활 치료 경과를 확인해 보죠.　　　　Let's check your progress of rehabilitation next week.

유진은 수술 후 회복이 잘 되었다는 소식을 듣고 감사했습니다.
Eugene was grateful to hear that his postoperative recovery has been great.

항암 치료를 받다
receive treatments
[get treated] for cancer

화학 요법을 받다
get [undergo, receive]
chemotherapy

깁스를 하다
wear a cast

침을 맞다
get acupuncture,
get ~ treated with
acupuncture, be treated
with acupuncture

~에 붕대를 감다
put a bandage on ~,
bandage one's ~

상처를 소독하다
disinfect one's
wound

~를 전신 마취하다
put ~ under
general anesthesia

~를 부분[국소] 마취하다
put ~ under local
[regional] anesthesia

상담 치료를 받다
receive counseling
therapy [treatment]

(신장) 투석을 하다
be put on (kidney)
dialysis

~를 절단하다
amputate
one's ~

휠체어를 타다
be in a
wheelchair

SENTENCES TO USE

저희 할머니는 손목에 침을 맞으시곤 했습니다.
My grandmother used to get her wrist treated with acupuncture.

붕대를 감기 전에 그 상처를 소독합시다.
Let's disinfect that wound before we bandage it.

전신 마취는 필요 없고, 국소 마취면 충분할 겁니다.
There is no need to put her under general anesthesia, simple local anesthesia will suffice.

따님이 스트레스를 많이 받는 것 같으니 상담 치료를 받아 보는 게 좋겠습니다.
Your daughter better go to counseling therapy since she seems to be under a lot of stress.

의무병은 전쟁터에서 군인의 다리를 절단하는 것 외에는 선택의 여지가 없었습니다.
The medic had no choice but to amputate the soldier's leg on the battle field.

MP3 **064**

119를 부르다
call 119

인공호흡을 하다
give
mouth-to-mouth
[a kiss of life]

심폐소생술을 하다
do [perform, give]
CPR (cardiopulmonary
resuscitation)

산소호흡기를 대다
put on an oxygen
respirator [a ventilator]

~ 흡입기를 사용하다
use a ~ inhaler
[puffer]

지혈하다
stop the
bleeding

~를 주무르다
massage [rub
down] one's ~

의식을 잃다
lose one's consciousness, go
black, pass [black] out, faint

의식을 회복하다(되찾다)
regain [recover] one's
consciousness

자동제세동기를 사용하다
use an AED (automated
external defibrillator) device

구급차를 타고 응급실에 가다
go to the ER (emergency room) by
ambulance [in an ambulance]

SENTENCES TO USE

아이에게 심폐소생술 하는 법을 배우는 것이 중요합니다.
It is important to learn how to perform CPR on a child.

제니는 천식 발작에 대비해 항상 흡입기를 가지고 다닙니다.
Jenny always carries an inhaler in case of an asthma attack.

봉합하기 전에 지혈을 해야 합니다.
I need to stop the bleeding before I can stitch it up.

제임스는 응급실로 가는 도중에 구급차 안에서 기절했습니다.
James passed out in the ambulance on the way to the ER.

온몸을 마사지하면 의식을 되찾는 데 도움이 됩니다.
Massaging one's whole body helps them regain consciousness.

약사에게 처방전을 제출하다
hand in [give]
a prescription to
a pharmacist

약의 효능을 묻다
inquire [ask] about
the effectiveness
[effect] of a medicine

복약 주기를 확인하다
check the
medication cycle

상비약을 구입하다
buy a household
medicine

약값을 결제하다
pay for a medicine
[meds]

건강 보조제에 관해 약사와 상담하다
consult a pharmacist on
a health supplement

가루약으로 조제를 요청하다
ask for powdered medicine,
ask to prepare powdered medicine

복용법 설명을 듣다
get an explanation
of how to take the
medicine

Side Effect

약사에게 부작용에 대한 설명을 듣다
have a pharmacist explain the
side effects, listen to a pharmacist
explaining the side effects

24
PHARMACY

24시간 문 여는 약국을 찾아가다
visit [go to] a pharmacy
open 24 hours a day

SENTENCES TO USE

약사에게 처방전 줄 때 부작용에 관해 물어보는 게 어때요?
Why don't you ask about the side effects when you give the prescription to the pharmacists?

비상시를 대비해 가정상비약을 몇 가지 사야 합니다.
I need to buy several household medicines in case of emergency.

아기들과 유아들은 알약을 삼키기 힘들어서 가루약을 복용합니다.
Babies and toddlers take powdered medicine because it's hard for them to swallow pills.

현재 복용 중인 약 때문에 건강 보조식품 복용은 약사와 먼저 상담을 해야 합니다.
You need to consult a pharmacist first on taking health supplements due to your current medication.

24시간 열고 주말에도 영업하는 약국을 찾았습니다!
I found a pharmacy that opens 24 hours and even on the weekends!

CHAPTER

8

은행

BANK

은행

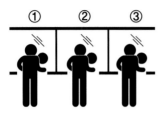

창구 대기자 수를 확인하다
check the number of people waiting
[waiting list] at the counter

번호표를 받고 순서를 기다리다
wait for one's turn after taking a number
[getting a number ticket]

~로 본인 인증을 하다
verify oneself through [with] ~,
confirm one's identification through ~

ATM에서 현금을 인출하다
withdraw cash
from an ATM

은행 계좌를 해지하다
close a bank account

입출금/적금 계좌를 만들다
set up [open] a deposit account / an installment savings account

SENTENCES TO USE

ATM기 보여요? 제가 현금을 좀 인출해야 해서요.
Do you see an ATM? I have to withdraw some cash.

밀라는 은행 계좌를 해지하기 위해 사진이 들어간 신분증으로 본인 인증을 했습니다.
In order to close her bank account, Mila verified herself through a photo ID.

돈을 저금하다/인출하다/송금하다
save / withdraw / transfer money

적립식 펀드에 가입하다
subscribe to an installment fund

지폐를 동전으로 바꾸다
change a bill into coins,
break a bill into coins

통장 정리를 하다
update one's
bankbook

환전을 하다
exchange money

세금/공과금을 내다
pay taxes / bills

대여 금고를 갖다
have [get] a safe-deposit
[safety-deposit] box

마이클은 적립식 펀드에 가입하기 전에 은행 과장과 상의할 것입니다.
Michael will consult a bank manager before he subscribes to an installment fund.

우리 부모님은 몇 년 동안 통장 정리를 안 하셨어요.
My parents have not updated their bankbook in years.

이런, 은행에서 미리 환전한다는 걸 깜빡했어!
Oh no, I forgot to exchange money at the bank beforehand!

온라인 뱅킹

은행 홈페이지에 접속하다
log in [on] to the bank website

모바일 뱅킹 앱을 열다
open the mobile banking app [bank app]

공인인증서를 발급하다/갱신하다/변경하다
issue / renew / change an authentication certificate

타 기관 공인인증서를 등록하다
register an authentication certificate from another agency

모바일 인증서를 내보내다/복사하다
export / copy mobile certificates

지문으로/비밀번호로/패턴 암호로 로그인하다
enter [use] a fingerprint /
a password / a pattern to log in

SENTENCES TO USE

댄은 한동안 모바일 뱅킹 앱을 열지 않아서 사용 전에 업그레이드를 해야 합니다.
Dan has not opened his mobile banking app for a while, so he has to upgrade it before using it.

1년에 한 번, 공인인증서를 갱신해야 합니다.
I have to renew an authentication certificate once a year.

거래를 원하는 계좌를 선택하다
select [choose] the account you
want to transact with

입금/출금/송금 거래를 선택하다
select [choose] a deposit / withdrawal /
transfer [remit] transaction

금액을 입력하다
enter one's amount

비밀번호/OTP 번호를 입력하다
enter a password /
an OTP (one-time programmable) number

잔액을 확인하다
check one's balance

온라인 계좌를 만들다
create [make] an online [a mobile] account

앗! 출금 대신 입금 거래를 선택했어요!
Oops! I chose a deposit transaction instead of withdrawal!

비밀번호를 여러 번 잘못 입력했더니 제 계좌가 잠겼습니다.
I entered a wrong password several times and now my account is locked.

제 잔액을 확인해 봤는데 월급이 입금되지 않았습니다.
I checked my balance and my monthly salary has not been deposited.

그녀는 주식 거래를 위해 온라인 계좌를 만들었습니다.
She made an online account for stock trading purposes.

LOAN

대출을 신청하다
apply for a loan

대출 심사를 받다
undergo a loan prequalification,
get prequalified for a loan

개인 신용 정보를 조회하다
check [undergo] one's
personal credit information

이자율을 확인하다
check [review] the interest rate

대출 약정서를 작성하다
draw up [fill in] a loan agreement

담보를 설정하다
set up a security
[collateral for a loan]

연대 보증을 서다
give joint surety,
underwrite one's debt [loan]

차용증을 작성하다
draw [write] up
a promissory note [an IOU]

SENTENCES TO USE

저희가 아무리 고객님 개인 신용 정보를 확인해도 고객님은 대출 자격이 안 됩니다.
No matter how many times we check your personal credit information, you are not
qualified for a loan.

대출 약정서를 작성하기 전에 제가 이자율을 확인할 것입니다.
I am going to check the interest rate before filling in a loan agreement.

가족이라고 해도 연대 보증을 서는 건 현명하지 못한 행동입니다.
It is unwise to underwrite one's debts even if it's for a family.

대출 상환 일정을 잡다
schedule repayment
[pay-back] of a loan

대출의 원금을/이자를 상환하다
repay [pay back] the principal /
interest of one's loan

금리 인하를 요구하다
demand an interest rate cut,
demand for a cut in interest rates

파산 신청을 하다
file for
bankruptcy

빚더미에 앉다(허덕이다)
drown in debt, be up to one's
ears in debt, be in a huge debt

주택 담보 대출을 받다
take out a mortgage (loan)

변동 금리/고정 금리로 주택 담보 대출을 받다
take out a variable [floating]-rate /
fixed-rate mortgage (loan)

주택 융자를 상환하려면 매달 원금과 이자를 얼마나 내야 하나요?
How much do I pay in principal and interest every month for our mortgage payment?

저 회사는 빚더미에 허덕이고 있어서 너 그곳에서 일하면 안 돼.
You should not work there since that company is drowning in debt.

A 안녕하세요. 송금하려고요.
▶ Hello. I'd like to transfer some money.

B 안녕하세요 고객님. 우선 본인 인증을 위해 신분증 확인하겠습니다.
● Good afternoon, sir. First, I would like to confirm your identification with an ID.

A 네, 신분증 여기 있습니다.
▶ Yes, here it is.

B 감사합니다. 본인 확인되셨습니다.
● Thank you, it's been confirmed.

여기 적혀 있는 계좌로 2,000달러 송금해 드리면 될까요?
● Should I help you transfer two thousand dollars to the account written here?

A 네. 계좌 잔액이 얼마죠?
▶ Yes, please. How much balance do I have in my account?

B 송금 후 잔액은 4,500달러입니다.
● Your balance will be at 4,500 dollars after the transfer.

A 감사합니다. 그리고 대출 상담도 받으려고 하는데요.
▶ Thank you. And I'd like to get a loan consultation please.

B 네, 고객님. 얼마 정도 대출이 필요하신가요?
● Yes, sir. How much loan are you in need?

A 개인 신용 대출로 3만 달러 받으려고 합니다. 금리가 얼마나 되죠?
▶ I'd like to take 30,000 dollars on a personal credit loan. What is the interest rate?

B 네, 금리는 개인 신용 정보 조회 후에 자세히 안내해 드릴 수 있습니다.
● No problem. We can inform you of the details of the interest rate after checking your personal credit information.

동의서 작성해 주시겠어요?
● Could you fill out the consent form?

A 여기 이름 적고 서명하면 되는 거죠?
▶ Do I sign here with my name on it?

B 맞습니다. (신용 조회) 평가 결과를 보니까 저희 은행 VIP이시긴 한데 신용 등급이 조금 낮아서 대출 한도액은 2만 달러, 이자율은 7.2%가 나옵니다.

🔴 That is correct. According to the result, you are our bank VIP with a low credit rating, so the loan limit is 20,000 dollars and the interest rate will be 7.2%.

A 7.2%요? 생각보다 높네요. 이자율을 낮출 방법이 있나요?

▶ 7.2%? That's higher than I expected. Is there any way to lower the interest rate?

B 저희 은행 개인 계좌로 급여 이체 계좌를 설정하시면 0.3%, 제휴 신용카드 사용 실적 월 300달러 이상 이용 실적이 있으시니 0.2%를 할인받게 됩니다.

🔴 If you set up a payroll transfer account with our personal account, you will receive 0.3%, using more than 300 dollars per month for affiliated credit card usage will get you 0.2%.

저희 은행 청약 통장 납입 실적이 있으시니, 0.2% 추가 우대 금리를 받으셔서 최종 이자율이 6.5%가 됩니다.

🔴 Since you have our bank's subscription account, you will receive an additional 0.2%, which will make the final interest rate 6.5%.

A 그럼 그렇게 2만 달러 대출, 24월 만기 종료 후 전액 상환, 이율 6.5%로 진행해 주세요.

▶ Then, please proceed with a 20,000-dollar loan and full repayment after 24 months at an interest rate of 6.5%.

중도 상환 수수료도 있나요?

▶ Is there an early redemption charge?

B 중도 상환 수수료는 없으니, 약정 종료 전이라도 원하시는 만큼 상환하시면 됩니다.

🔴 There is no early redemption charge, you can repay as much as you want before the end of the contract.

대출 거래 약정서 여기 있고요. 대출금은 1시간 내로 고객님 계좌로 입금됩니다. 감사합니다.

🔴 Here's the transaction agreement. The loan will be deposited into your account within an hour. Thank you.

구청 & 행정복지센터

민원을 넣다
put in [file]
a civil complaint

주민등록등본을 발급받다
get a copy of one's resident
registration issued

여권을 신청하다
apply for
a passport

장애인 등록 신청을 하다
apply for the disability registration,
get registered as disable

주민등록증을 재발급받다
get one's resident
registration card reissued

관공서에 전입신고를 하다
notify the public office of the new address (that one has
moved to), give the public office a moving-in notification

SENTENCES TO USE

아버지가 공영 주차 공간 부족에 분노하셔서 민원을 넣으셨습니다.
My father was furious about the lack of public parking spaces, so he put in a civil
complaint.

해외여행 전에 저 여권을 새로 신청해야 해요.
I need to apply for a new passport before our travel overseas.

저 남자분 장애인 등록이랑 장애인 주차증 신청하는 것 좀 도와주시겠어요?
Could you help that man with his application for the disability registration and a disabled
parking badge?

혼인/출생/사망 신고를 하다
register [report] one's marriage / birth / death

정부 보조금을 신청하다
apply for a
government subsidy

정부 정책 설명회를 듣다
listen to a government policy
briefing [briefing session]

사업자 등록증을 신청하다
apply for a
business license

가족관계증명서를 발급받다
get a family relation certificate
[a certificate of family relation] issued

혼인 신고를 한 게 엊그제 같은데, 이제 우리 아들 출생 신고를 하러 왔네요.
It seems like we registered our marriage only a few days ago, but now we came to report our son's birth.

오웬은 식당을 열기 전에 구청에 사업자 등록증을 신청해야 했습니다.
Owen had to apply for a business license at the ward office before he could open his restaurant.

우표를 구매하다
buy [purchase] a stamp

편지를/우편물을/택배를 보내다
send a letter / mail / a parcel [a package]

등기 우편으로 보내다
send by
registered mail

편지를 우체통에 넣다
put a letter in the
mailbox

~를 속달로 보내다
send ~ through [by] express
[special delivery]

해외 택배를 보내다
send an overseas parcel

~을 항공편으로 보내다
send ~ by air mail
[air, plane]

SENTENCES TO USE

저는 해외 유학 시절 한국으로 국제 택배를 보내곤 했습니다.
When I was studying abroad, I used to send international parcels to Korea.

등기 우편은 배달 시 바로 서명하셔야 합니다.
You need to sign the registered mail upon its delivery.

소포를 항공편으로 보내는 것보다 배로 보내는 것이 더 오래 걸립니다.
It takes longer to ship a parcel by sea mail compared to sending by airmail.

~을 배편으로 보내다
ship [send] ~ by sea mail,
send ~ by ship [sea]

우편 사서함을 이용하다
use a P. O. Box
(post office box)

우체국 보험에 가입하다
take out post office
insurance, take up a post
office insurance policy

우체부가 ~를 배달하다
a postman delivers ~

EMS로 ~을 보내다
send ~ by EMS
(Express Mail Service)

규격 봉투/상자를 구매하다
buy [purchase] a standard
envelope / box

익일 배송/당일 배송을 요청하다
request next-day / same-
day delivery

제이슨은 주소지가 불규칙해서 우편 사서함을 이용했습니다.
Jason used a P. O. Box due to his irregular place of address.

어머니가 저를 위해 우체국 보험에 가입해 주셨습니다.
My mother took out post office insurance for me.

A 대기 번호 331번 고객님,
2번 창구로 와 주세요.
▶ Waiting number 331, please
come to window #2.

B 안녕하세요. 이 우편물 두 개를
등기 우편으로 보내려고요.
● Hello, I'd like to send these
two by registered mail.

A 네, 고객님. 등기로 보내실 것
하나씩 저울에 올려놔 주세요.
▶ No problem. Please put
each mail you want to send on
the scale.

일반 등기로 하면 총 4달러이고,
배송까지 2~3일 걸립니다.
▶ It's 4 dollars in total by
general registered mail which
takes 2-3 days to deliver.

익일 특급으로 하면 총 6달러이고
내일까지 배송이 보장됩니다.
▶ And if you use express mail,
it's 6 dollars with guaranteed
delivery tomorrow.

B 그럼 익일 특급으로 해 주세요.
● Then I will proceed with the
express delivery.

A 알겠습니다. 수신자 주소와
연락처를 잘 보이게 기재해 주세요.
▶ Okay. Please write down the
recipient's address and contact
information clearly.

B 그리고 이 상자도 뉴욕에
택배 보내려고 하는데요.
● And I'd like to send this box
to New York, please.

A 혹시 안에 인화성 물질이나 잘
부서지는 물건 또는 상할 수 있는
음식류가 있나요?
▶ Is there any flammable
substance, fragile item, or food
that can go bad in the box?

B 아니요. 이건 그냥 책이에요.
● No. These are just books.

A 박스 무게가 30kg을 넘어서 배송이 불가능합니다.

▶ The box weighs more than 30kg, so it cannot be delivered.

불편하시겠지만 박스 두 개로 나누어 포장해서 배송하셔야겠어요.

▶ I know it's inconvenient, but you need to repackage it into two boxes to deliver it.

(10분 후에 Ten minutes later)

B 두 개로 다시 포장했어요.

● I repackaged it in two.

A 고객님, 배송이 약 3일 걸리는 일반 배송은 한 박스에 5달러이고 익일 배송이 되는 속달은 한 박스에 9달러인데 어떤 것으로 해 드릴까요?

▶ The regular delivery takes about 3 days and is 5 dollars per box, and the express delivery is 9 dollars per box and will be delivered the next day. Which one would you like?

B 일반 배송으로 부탁드려요.

● I'll use the regular delivery service.

A 전체 금액은 22달러입니다.

▶ The total amount is 22 dollars.

카드는 앞에 있는 리더기에 꽂아 주세요.

▶ Please insert the card to the reader in front of you.

영수증 필요하세요?

▶ Do you need a receipt?

B 네, 주세요. 감사합니다.

● Yes, please. Thank you.

CHAPTER

쇼핑

SHOPPING

쇼핑몰, 마트 & 시장

쇼핑 목록을 만들다/
쇼핑 목록에 ~을 넣다
make one's shopping list /
put ~ on one's shopping list

쇼핑 카트/쇼핑 바구니를 꺼내다
take [pull] out a shopping
cart / a shopping basket

물건을 고르다
choose goods

~ 가격을 문의하다
ask the price of ~

~의 가격을 비교하다
compare prices

시식 코너에서 제품 맛을 보다
taste [sample, try] a product
at the free-sample stand [booth],
try a free-sample at the booth

SENTENCES TO USE

아, 쇼핑 목록에 우유와 계란 넣는 걸 깜빡했네요.
Oh, I forgot to put milk and eggs on the shopping list.

우리 어머니는 시장에서 물건을 고르기 전에 가격을 비교합니다.
My mother compares prices before choosing goods at the market.

바이올렛은 시식 코너에서 시식을 해 보고 제품을 카트에 담았습니다.
Violet tried a free-sample at the booth and put the products in her cart.

~을 카트/바구니에 담다
put ~ in a cart / a basket

가격을 흥정하다
bargain [haggle] with someone over the price

~을 덤으로 주다
throw in ~ / throw ~ in

셀프 계산대를 이용하다
use a self-checkout counter [self-checkout]

계산대에 물건들을 올리다
put things on the counter
[checkstand, register]

제가 이 토마토소스 사면 파스타 한 팩 덤으로 주실 수 있나요?
Can you throw in a pack of pasta for free if I buy this tomato sauce?

줄 서기 싫으면 셀프 계산대를 이용하시면 됩니다.
If you don't want to stand in line, you can use the self-checkout counter.

무빙워크를 이용하다
use a moving walkway [sidewalk]

음식물 쓰레기 봉투를 사다
buy a food waste bag

쇼핑백에 ~을 담다
put ~ in one's shopping bag

포인트를 적립하다
earn [collect]
reward points

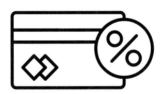

제휴카드로 할인을 받다
get a discount with a partner membership card

SENTENCES TO USE

데이나는 카트를 제자리로 갖다 놓으려고 무빙워크를 이용했습니다.
Dana used a moving walkway to put her cart back in place.

식료품을 쇼핑백에 넣어서 집으로 가져오는 데 당신 도움이 필요합니다.
I need your help putting my groceries in my shopping bag and bringing it back home.

저울에 ~ 무게를 재다
weigh ~ on a scale

카트를 제자리에 가져다 놓다
put [return] the cart back in place

고객센터에 항의하다
complain to the customer center,
bring up an issue with the customer center

고객센터에 가서 사은품을 받다
go to the customer center and
get a giveaway [a free gift]

구입한 물건을 차 트렁크에 싣다
put the purchased goods [items] in the trunk,
load the trunk with purchased goods [items]

구입한 물건을 배달시키다
have the purchased
goods [items] delivered

저울에 무게를 재기 전에 양상추를 비닐봉지에 넣으세요.
Put the lettuce in a plastic bag before you weigh it on a scale.

고객센터에 가서 사은품으로 세제 받는 것 잊지 마세요.
Don't forget to go to the customer center and get a detergent as a free gift.

저 노부인이 트렁크에 식료품 싣는 것 좀 도와줄 직원을 불러 주시겠어요?
Could you get a staff to help that elderly lady to put her grocery in the trunk?

UNIT 2 계산 & 결제

바코드를 스캔하다
scan the bar code

카드 할부 거래를 요청하다
make a monthly credit card installment transaction [plan]

일시불로 결제하다
pay in a lump sum, pay in full

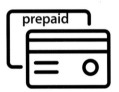

선불카드로 결제하다
pay with [use] one's prepaid card

현금으로 결제하다
pay in cash

거스름돈을 세다
count out one's change

현금영수증을 요청하다
ask for a cash receipt

SENTENCES TO USE

4개월 무이자 할부로 결제하고 싶습니다.
I'd like to pay in an interest-free 4 month installment plan.

에단은 신용카드로 결제했는데 자신도 모르게 현금영수증을 달라고 했습니다.
Ethan unknowingly asked for a cash receipt when he paid with a credit card.

MP3 075

상품권으로 결제하다
pay with a gift certificate (card)

계산대 점원에게 카드를 건네다
give [hand] one's card to the cashier

카드 리더기에 서명을 하다
sign a card reader

(계산대 점원이) 영수증과 함께 카드를 돌려주다
return [give back] the card with the receipt

핸드폰으로 전자카드를 켜다
turn on an electronic card
with one's mobile phone

핸드폰을 스캐너에 대고
금액을 지불하다
scan one's phone to pay
[make a payment]

리더기에 카드를 꽂다
insert the card into
the reader

현금 결제를 취소하고 상품권으로 결제할 수 있나요?
Can I cancel my cash payment and pay with a gift certificate instead?

아, 스마일페이 있으세요? 고객님 핸드폰을 여기에 스캔해서 결제해 주세요.
Oh, you have Smile Pay? Please scan your phone here to make a payment.

저에게 카드 안 주셔도 되고요, 바로 앞에 있는 리더기에 카드 꽂으시면 됩니다.
You don't need to hand me the card, you can insert the card into the reader right in front
of you.

A 지금부터 10명에 한해서 신선하고
맛있는 국내산 양념 소갈비를
한 팩당 10달러에 드립니다!

▶ Starting now, we are offering
fresh and delicious marinated
domestic beef ribs for 10 dollars
per pack for only 10 people!

1인당 최대 3팩까지만 드리니
서둘러서 구입하세요.

▶ We only allow a maximum of 3
packs per person, so hurry up.

B 저 양념 갈비 두 팩 주세요!

● I'll take 2 packs of marinated
ribs!

오늘 어떤 돼지고기가 좋아요?

● What pork is good today?

A 네, (양념 소갈비) 여기 있습니다.
버크셔산 흑돼지 삼겹살이 어제
온 거라 아주 신선하고요.

▶ Here you go. The black pork
belly from Berkshire just came in
yesterday, so it's very fresh.

오늘까지 특가로 20% 할인해
드리고 있으니 쌀 때 가져가세요.

▶ It's on a special 20% discount
until today. So, you better take it
when it's cheap.

B 그럼, 흑돼지 삼겹살도 두 팩 주세요.

● Then I will take 2 packs of black
pork belly, too.

생선은 어떤 게 제철인가요?

● Which fish is in season?

A 지금 고등어가 제철이라 살이
올라서 맛있습니다.

▶ Mackerel is in season, so it's
fattened up and delicious.

원래 한 마리에 10달러인데요. 지금
1+1 이벤트 진행 중입니다.

▶ It's usually 10 dollars for one,
but we are currently having a 1+1
event.

B 그것도 주세요.

● I'll take it as well.

해물탕 밀키트 종류가 많은 것
같은데 하나 추천해 주시겠어요?

● There seem to be many kinds
of spicy seafood stew meal kits,
can you recommend one?

A 얼큰한 걸 좋아하시면 오징어와
홍합이 많이 들어간 이 제품을
추천드리고요.

▶ If you like spicy food,
I recommend this one with a lot
of squid and mussels.

시원한 맛을 원하시면 바다게와
낙지가 많이 들어가 있는 제품이
있습니다.

▶ If you like savory flavor, there is
also a product with a lot of blue
crabs and small octopus.

가격은 2배 차이 나지만 구성이
아주 좋아서 많이 사가세요.

▶ The price is double, but
it's popular because of the
composition of the kit.

B 바다게가 들어간 제품은 비싸서
다음에 사는 걸로 할게요.

● The kit with the blue crab is out
of my price range, so I'll get it next
time.

계산할게요. 50달러 이상 구매 시
3달러 할인 쿠폰을 문자로 받았는데
할인 적용해 주세요.

● I'd like to pay for my groceries,
and I want to use this 3-dollar
discount coupon for purchases
over 50 dollars through text.

A 네, 쿠폰 적용해서 65달러입니다.
비닐봉투 필요하세요? 봉투는
별도로 10센트 내셔야 해요.

▶ Yes, it's 65 dollars with the
coupon applied. Do you need a
plastic bag? It's 10 cents extra.

B 괜찮습니다. 장바구니 가져와서요.
어떤 카드가 무이자 할부가 되나요?

● That's okay. I brought my
own shopping bag. What card is
interest-free?

A YXZ 카드로 결제하시면 6개월까지
무이자 가능하세요.

▶ You can get up to 6-month
interest-free with a YXZ credit
card.

B 3개월 무이자로 해 주세요.
영수증은 버려 주시고요.

● I'd like to pay in a 3-month
interest-free installment plan.
You can throw the receipt away.

A 네, 포인트 적립은 어떻게
해드릴까요?

▶ Yes, how would you like your
frequency points?

B 전화번호 뒤 네 자리 0355, 킴벌리
헤이즈로 적립해 주세요. 이거
배달되는 거죠?

● Please put the points under
the last four digits of my phone
number which is 0355 Kimberly
Hays. Can I get my groceries
delivered?

A 네, 여기에 주소 적어 주시면
30분 내로 댁에서 받으실 거예요.

▶ Yes. If you write down your
address here, you will receive
your groceries at home within 30
minutes.

B 네, 감사합니다.

● Okay, thank you.

백화점/쇼핑몰/아웃렛에 가다
go to a department store / a shopping mall / an outlet

~를 위해 여기저기 둘러보다
shop around for ~

아이쇼핑하다
go window-shopping

흥청망청 (마구) 쇼핑하다
go on a shopping [spending] spree

~ 매장에 들어가다
go into a ~ store

~의 상태를 확인하다
check the condition [state] of ~

사이즈를 문의하다
ask about the size

(탈의실에서) ~을 입어 보다, 신어 보다, 착용해 보다
try on ~, try ~ on
(in the fitting/dressing room)

가격을 확인하다
check the price

~의 재고를 확인하다
check for ~'s inventory, check [find out] if ~ is in stock

완판되다
be sold out

신상이 입고되다
be stocked with new products, be new in stock

거울로 자신을 확인하다
check oneself in the mirror

SENTENCES TO USE

클라라는 지갑을 사러 백화점에 갔지만 결국 아이쇼핑만 하게 됐습니다.
Clara went to a department store to buy a purse but ended up window-shopping.

아웃렛에 가서 어떤 신상이 입고됐는지 확인해 봐요.
Let's go to the outlet to check out what's new in stock.

우리 가족은 계절마다 쇼핑을 왕창 합니다.
My family goes on a shopping spree every season.

신발 가게에 들어가서 점원에게 한정판 신발 재고가 있는지 물어봤습니다.
I walked into a shoe store and asked the clerk if they had a limited edition shoe on stock.

이 셔츠와 바지 입어 봐도 되나요?
Can I please try this shirt and pants on?

할인 판매 상품을 찾아보다
look for bargains,
look for merchandise
on sale

치수를 재다
take (one's)
measurements

~을 다른 색상으로/
사이즈로 찾아보다
look for ~ in
a different color / size

줄 서서 기다리다/
일렬로 서다
wait / stand in line

현금 할인이 있는지
물어보다
ask if there is a
cash discount

덜 비싼 것으로 구매하다
buy something less
expensive [pricey]

배달이 가능한지 묻다
ask [check] if delivery
is possible

주차(할인)권을 받다
get one's parking
validated, get a parking
voucher [discount]

환불 규정 설명을 듣다
get [listen to] an
explanation of the
refund policy

쇼핑백을
하나 더 달라고 하다
ask for [request]
another shopping bag

품질 보증카드가
달려오다
come with a
guarantee card

품질 보증서가 포함돼
있는지 확인하다
ask [check] if the warranty
[guarantee] is included

SENTENCES TO USE

파이퍼는 판매원에게 더 작은 사이즈 드레스를 찾아달라고 부탁했습니다.
Piper asked the sales clerk to look for the dress in a smaller size.

계산대에서 줄 서서 기다립시다.　　　　　　　　　　Let's wait in line at the check-out counter.

가끔 200달러 이상 결제하면 몇몇 가게가 배달해 주기도 하니까 배달이 가능한지 점원에게 물어보는 게 좋을 것 같아요.
Sometimes some stores deliver when you pay over $200, so you might want to ask the clerk
if delivery is possible.

핀은 쇼핑백 하나 더 달라고 요청하기 전에 주차권을 받고 싶었습니다.
Finn wanted to get his parking validated before he could ask for another shopping bag.

이 가방이 품질 보증 카드가 달려오는지 확인해 줄래요?
Can you check if this bag comes with a guarantee card?

온라인 쇼핑

온라인 쇼핑을 하다
shop online

~에서 주문하다
order at
[from] ~

~을 선주문(사전 예약 주문)하다
pre-order ~, put ~ in a
pre-order request

제품/가격을 비교하다
compare goods /
prices

~를 장바구니에 넣다
add ~ to one's shopping
[check-out] list

~를 관심 품목 리스트에
추가하다(찜하다)
add ~ to one's wish list

할인 쿠폰을 적용하다
apply a discount
coupon

배송비를 지불하다
pay for delivery
[shipping]

배송 주소를 입력하다
enter one's shipping
address

안심 번호를 사용하다
use a "safe number"
[a virtual number, a
temporary phone
number]

공동 구매를 하다
make a joint purchase,
put in a joint order

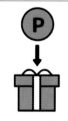

포인트를 사용하다
use bonus
[reward] points

SENTENCES TO USE

저번에 온라인 쇼핑할 때 제가 실수로 이전 주소를 입력했어요.
Last time I shopped online, I accidentally entered my previous address.

저는 사전 주문한 최신 휴대폰을 배송받았어요.
I received the latest mobile phone that I pre-ordered.

제나는 나중에 선택할 수 있게 조카 생일 선물을 관심 품목 리스트에 추가했습니다.
Jena added her nephew's birthday gifts to her wishlist to choose later.

그는 배송비 할인 쿠폰을 적용할 수 없어서 온라인 쇼핑몰에 화가 났습니다.   He was mad at the online mall
for not being able to apply a discount coupon for the shipping fee.

저는 신원 도용 방지를 위해 배송에 항상 안심 번호를 사용합니다.
I always use a virtual number for my shipping to avoid identity theft.

해외 직구를 하다
make a direct overseas purchase,
purchase overseas

해외 구매 대행을 이용하다
use [buy through] an overseas
purchasing agent

개인통관고유부호를 입력하다
enter one's PCCC (personal
customs clearance code)

주문 내역을 조회하다
check the details
of an order

배송 정보를 조회하다
check the tracking
information

판매자에게
문의 글을 남기다
leave [post] a
question to the seller

배송 지연으로
판매자에게 항의하다
complain to the seller
about delayed delivery

부분 배송을 받다
get [receive] a partial
shipment

A를 B로 교환하다
exchange A for B

~을 반품하다
return ~

사진과 함께 후기를 올리다
post [write] a review
with a photo

SENTENCES TO USE

해외 구매를 할 때마다 전 배송 지연으로 판매자에게 항의해야 해요.
Every time I purchase overseas, I have to complain to the seller about the delayed delivery.

잘못 주문하신 것 같으면 주문 내역을 확인하셔야 합니다.
You need to check the details of your order if you feel like you ordered something wrong.

판매자에게 배송 문의를 남기기 전에 배송 정보 조회를 해 주세요.
Please check the tracking information before leaving a delivery question to the seller.

아이리스는 크리스마스 쇼핑 물품 중 일부 배송을 받았고, 지금은 다른 소포가 도착하기를 기다리고 있습니다.   Iris received a partial shipment of her Christmas shopping and she is waiting for another package to arrive.

수잔은 판매자에게 그녀가 산 불량 청바지를 짧은 치마로 교환해 달라고 요청했습니다.
Susan asked the seller to exchange her faulty jeans for a short skirt.

10

활동

ACTIVITIES

사교 모임

Welcome!

~를 사교 모임에 초대하다
invite ~ to a social gathering [event, party]

오픈 채팅 그룹에 참여하다
join an open chat group

주식 투자 모임에 참여하다
participate in a stock investment meeting

스터디 그룹에 참여하다
join a study group

파티에 참석하다
attend a party

와인 시음회에 가다
go to a wine tasting

SENTENCES TO USE

저는 작년에 사교 행사에 초대받았지만, 내향적 인간이라서 가지는 않았습니다.
I was invited to a social event last year, but I did not go because I am an introvert.

저는 주식 투자 모임에서 굉장히 좋은 팁을 몇 개 받았습니다.
I received some great tips at the stock investment meeting.

동네 ~ 소모임에 가입하다
join a small local ~ group

친목회를 결성하다
form a social meeting [a get-together]

동창회에 나가다
attend [go to] one's school reunion,
go to an alumni reunion [meeting]

서로 번호를 교환하다
exchange
(phone) numbers

가까운 지인들과 요리 교실에 나가다
go to a cooking class with close
acquaintances

다과회를 즐기다
enjoy a(n) (afternoon) tea party

플로라는 어제 동네 볼링 모임에 가입했는데 분위기를 마음에 들어합니다.
Flora joined a local bowling group yesterday and she likes the atmosphere.

그는 첫사랑을 만나러 학교 동창회에 나갔습니다.
He went to his school reunion to meet his first love.

해나는 다과회를 즐긴 후 사람들과 전화번호를 교환했습니다.
Hannah exchanged phone numbers with people after enjoying a tea party.

A 친구에게 이야기 많이 들었어요. 만나서 반가워요.

▶ I've heard a lot from my friend. Nice to meet you.

B 그러세요? 저도 반갑습니다. 사진이랑 좀 달라 보이세요!

● Really? Nice to meet you, too. You look a little different from the picture!

물론 좋은 의미로요. 운동 많이 하시나 봐요.

● In a good way, of course. I guess you work out a lot.

A 고마워요. 그래 보일 수도 있어요.

▶ Thank you, it might look like that.

그 사진 찍은 이후로 운동을 정말 열심히 했거든요.

▶ I've been working hard since I took that picture.

취업하고 몸이 아프고 난 후에는 꾸준하게 건강 관리를 하고 있습니다.

▶ After getting a job and getting sick, I am continuously taking care of my health.

운동하는 건 좋아하세요?

▶ Do you like to work out?

B 네, 저도 요가와 필라테스를 꾸준히 하고 있어요.

● Yes, I do yoga and Pilates constantly.

등산도 한 달에 두 번씩은 가려고 합니다.

● I'm also trying to go hiking twice a month.

A 그러시군요. 뭐니 뭐니 해도 건강이 최고니까요.

▶ I see. Health is the most important thing.

평소에 퇴근하시고는 뭐 하세요?

▶ What do you usually do after work?

B 요리 학원에서 이탈리아 요리를 배우기도 하고 독서 모임도 나가요.

● I learn Italian cooking at the academy and also go to a book club.

매주 같이 책을 정해서 읽고 리뷰를 하는데 사람들마다 다양하게 내용을 해석하는 게 재미있더라고요.

● We read and review books together every week and it's fun to interpret it in various ways.

그쪽은요?

● What about you?

A 우와, 엄청 바쁘신 분 같아요!
▶ Wow, you sound like a busy person!

저는 주중에는 수영 레슨을 받고 헬스장에서 운동을 하고 있습니다.
▶ During the week, I take swimming lessons and work out at the gym.

얼마 전까지 보디 프로필 사진 찍는다고 일대일 PT를 매일 받았어요.
▶ Not too long ago, I got one-on-one personal training every day to take a body profile picture.

주말에는 집에서 쉬거나 친구들을 만납니다.
▶ On weekends, I rest at home or meet my friends.

제가 술을 안 마셔서, 술집보다는 주로 맛집을 찾아다니는 편이죠.
▶ I don't drink, so I usually look for good restaurants rather than bars.

B 대단하신데요. 저는 등산 가거나 재미있는 영화 있으면 보러 다녀요.
● That's amazing. I go hiking or watch movies if there is anything interesting.

A 그러시군요. 저도 자전거 동호회 회원들과 자전거를 타거나 등산을 자주 갑니다.
▶ I see. I often ride a bicycle with my cycle club members or go hiking.

저도 영화를 좋아해서 한 달에 두 번씩은 영화관에 가요.
▶ I also like movies, so I go to the movies twice a month.

다음에는 같이 영화 한 편 볼까요?
▶ Shall we watch a movie together next time?

B 좋아요! 영화 보고 맛집에서 맛있는 음식도 먹으면 좋겠네요.
● Great! I hope we can watch a movie and eat delicious food at a restaurant.

언젠가는 등산도 같이해 보고 말이에요.
● We can hike together someday, too.

A 아주 좋죠. 그러면 날짜를 한 번 잡아 보도록 해요.
▶ Very good. Then let's set a date.

UNIT **2** 영화관

영화 개봉 날짜를 확인하다
check the release date
of the movie

현재 상영 중인 영화를 찾아보다
look [search] for a movie that is currently
showing [playing, screening]

박스오피스 순위를 확인하다
check the box office ranking

매표소에서 영화 티켓을 구입하다
buy a movie ticket at the box office

인터넷으로 영화 티켓을 예매하다
book [reserve] a movie ticket online

좌석을 지정하다/예약하다
designate / reserve a seat

SENTENCES TO USE

빈스는 영화를 고르기 전에 항상 박스오피스 순위를 확인하고 예고편을 봅니다.
Vince always checks the box office ranking and watches the preview
before he chooses a movie.

써니는 현재 1위인 영화 좌석을 예약하지 않은 걸 후회했습니다.
Sunny regretted on not reserving a seat for a top ranking movie.

팝콘과 음료를 사다
buy popcorn and
drinks [beverages]

스마트폰을 무음으로 설정하다
set [put] one's smartphone on
mute [silent, silent mode]

영화 예고편을 보다
watch a movie preview [trailer]

영화를 보다/즐기다
watch / enjoy a movie

3D 영화를 보다
watch a 3D movie

평점과 리뷰를 남기다
leave [write] ratings and reviews

다니엘은 항상 간식을 가지고 오고, 극장에서 팝콘이나 음료수를 절대 사지 않습니다.
Daniel always brings his own snack and never buys popcorn or
drinks at movie theaters.

한번은 휴대폰을 무음 모드로 설정하는 걸 깜박했는데 영화 보는 도중에 휴대폰이 울렸어요!
One time, I forgot to set my phone on silent mode and it rang during a movie!

포인트를 받을 수 있어서 전 영화를 보고 나면 항상 평점과 리뷰를 남깁니다.
I always leave ratings and reviews after I watch a movie because I can earn points.

연극/뮤지컬을 보다
watch [see] a play /
a musical

버스킹(길거리) 공연을 보다
watch [see] a busking performance
[a street performance]

강연회를/포럼을 경청하다
listen to a lecture / a forum

전시회에 가다
go to an exhibition

손으로 도자기를 빚다
make pottery by hand

~ 공연/경연을 보다
watch a ~ performance / contest

SENTENCES TO USE

한 젊은 커플이 길거리 공연을 보려고 길가에 서 있었습니다.
A young couple stood by the road to watch a street performance.

저는 딸과 미술 전시회에 가서 엽서 만들기 체험을 했습니다.
I went to an art exhibition with my daughter and experienced making a postcard.

미란다는 손으로 도자기를 빚는 취미가 있습니다.
Miranda has a hobby of making pottery by hand.

당신 가족은 발레 공연 보는 걸 좋아하나요?
Does your family like watching a ballet performance?

문화센터에서 ~ 수업을 듣다
take a ~ class [lesson]
at a cultural center

시를 낭독하다
recite a poem [poetry],
read one's poetry aloud

~ 만들기 체험을 하다
experience making ~

독서 모임에 참여하다
participate in a reading
club [a book club]

복지관/주민센터에서 꽃꽂이를 배우다
take lessons in flower arrangement at
a welfare center / a community center

저희 할머니는 문화센터에서 탁구 수업을 들으세요.
My grandmother takes a table tennis lesson at a cultural center.

샘이 독서 모임에 참석해 시를 낭독한다니 믿기지 않습니다.
I can't believe that Sam participates in a reading club and reads his poetry aloud.

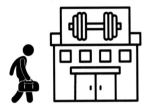

헬스장에 가다
go to the gym
[fitness center]

재등록을 하다
re-register

헬스장에 신규 등록을 하다
make a new registration at the gym,
get newly registered at the gym

운동복을 입다/운동복으로 갈아입다
put on [wear] / change into
one's sportswear

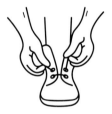

운동화를 신다
put on [wear] one's sneakers
[workout shoes]

운동 상담을 받다
get [receive]
exercise counseling

SENTENCES TO USE

그녀는 회원 재등록하려고 체육관에 갔습니다.
She went to the gym to re-register as a member.

단은 신규 등록한 지 얼마 안 돼서 자기 운동화를 신어야 하는 줄 몰랐습니다.
Don did not know he had to wear his own sneakers because he just got newly registered.

체지방 측정 전에 운동복으로 갈아입으시지요.
Why don't you change into your sportswear before we measure your body fat?

트레이너의 지도를 받다
be [get] coached by a trainer

체지방을 측정하다
measure one's body fat

운동하기 전에
스트레칭을 하다
stretch before
exercising
[a workout]

1:1 레슨을 받다
take [have] a one-on-one
[private] lesson

그룹 레슨을 받다
take [have]
a group lesson

땀 흘린 후 씻다
wash [clean] up after sweating

운동 전에 스트레칭을 하면 아무래도 부상을 예방할 수 있습니다.
It is likely that stretching before exercise prevents injury.

1:1 수업을 받을지 그룹 수업을 받을지 결정할 수 없다면 상담을 먼저 받으세요.
If you can't decide on taking a one-on-one lesson or a group lesson, get counseling first.

유산소 운동을 하다
do aerobic exercise,
do cardio (exercise)

러닝머신을 달리다
run on a treadmill

웨이트 트레이닝을 하다
do weight training

아령을 들다
lift dumbbells

에어로빅을 하다
do aerobics (dance)

트랙을 걷다/뛰다
walk / run the track

스쿼을 하다
do squats

격투기 훈련을 하다
train in martial arts

체력 단련을 하다
work on one's
physical strength

운동 기구를 사용하다
use the exercise
equipment

심호흡을 하다
take a deep
breath

마무리 운동을 하다
do a finishing
exercise

필라테스 레슨을 받다
get [take] a
Pilates lesson

SENTENCES TO USE

아령을 들면서 쉬운 웨이트 트레이닝을 해 봐요.
Let's do some easy weight training by lifting dumbbells.

오후에 에어로빅하는 여성분들 그룹이 여럿 있습니다.
There are several lady groups doing aerobics in the afternoon.

격투기 훈련을 하기 전에 체력을 단련해야 합니다.
You need to work on your physical strength before you can train in martial arts.

운동 기구 사용 전에 사용 설명서를 읽어 보시기 바랍니다.
Please read the instructions before using the exercise equipment.

스쿼하는 동안 심호흡을 하세요.
Take deep breathes in between squats.

구기 종목을 하다
play ball
games

육상 대회에 나가다
take part in a track and
field competition

조기 축구회에 가입하다
join [sign up for]
a morning soccer club

사회인 야구단에서 뛰다
play in the citizens
baseball league

판정승으로 이기다
win [score] a decision,
win by a decision

만장일치로 이기다
win by a unanimous vote [decision]

무승부 경기를 하다, 무승부로 끝나다
play to a draw,
result in [end in] a tie

반칙을 하다
commit
a foul

경고를 받다
get [receive]
a warning
[a yellow card]

판정에 불만을 제기하다
complain [file a complaint]
about a judgment [a ruling]

퇴장당하다
be [get] sent out of a game,
get [receive] a red card

SENTENCES TO USE

육상 경기에 참가해서 메달을 따는 건 큰 명예입니다.
It's a great honor to take part in a track and field competition and win a medal.

이 동네 조기 축구회에는 중년 남성들이 많습니다.
There are a lot of middle-aged men in this local morning soccer club.

제 남자 친구는 매주 토요일에 사회인 야구 리그에서 뜁니다.
My boyfriend plays in the citizens baseball league every Saturday.

경기에서 과도한 몸싸움은 경고로 이어질 수 있습니다.
Excessive tussles in a match can lead to getting warnings.

반칙을 너무 많이 하는 선수들은 퇴장당할 수 있습니다.
Athletes who commit too many fouls can get sent out of a game.

(실내) 암벽 등반을 하다
go (indoor)
rock climbing

산악자전거를 타다
ride a mountain bike

텐트를 치고 캠핑하다
pitch [set up, put up] a tent and camp

야외 바비큐를 하다
have an outdoor barbecue

낚시를 하다
go fishing

골프를 치다/스크린 골프를 치다
play golf / play indoor golf [golf simulator]

SENTENCES TO USE

요즘 많은 사람들이 실내 암벽 등반을 하러 갑니다.
A lot of people go indoor rock climbing these days.

야외를 사랑하는 사람들은 밖에서 텐트 치고 캠핑하는 것도 좋아하는 경향이 있습니다.
People who love outdoors also tend to like to pitch a tent and camp outside.

구명조끼 착용 후 물에서 수영하시거나 배낚시를 하시기 바랍니다.
Please put on a life vest before swimming in water or go fishing on a boat.

스키/스노보드를 타다
go skiing, ski / go
snowboarding, snowboard

요트를 타다
sail a yacht,
cruise in a yacht

수상스키를 타다
go water skiing

패러글라이딩을 하다
go paragliding, paraglide

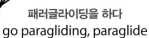

스카이다이빙을 하다
go skydiving, skydive

승마를 하다
go horseback [horse] riding

롤러스케이트/인라인스케이트를 타다
go roller-skate / in-line skating

스노보드 타러 갈 수 있는 겨울이 너무 기다려져요!
I can't wait for the winter when I can go snowboarding!

간 큰 사람들은 스카이다이빙이나 패러글라이딩 같은 극한 스포츠를 좋아합니다.
Daredevils love extreme sports like skydiving or paragliding.

11

자기 관리

SELF MANAGEMENT

미용실

미용실 예약을 하다
make a reservation [an appointment]
for a hair salon, make a hair appointment

가운을 걸치다
put on a gown

머리를 다듬다
get one's hair trimmed,
get a trim, trim one's hair

머리를 자르다
have [get] one's
hair cut, get a hair cut

머리숱을 치다
get one's hair thinned out,
thin out one's hair

이발기로 양옆 머리를 밀다
get one's sides shaved with a hair clipper,
shave one's sides with a hair clipper

파마하다
get a perm,
have one's hair permed

SENTENCES TO USE

그 미용실은 너무 유명해서 예약이 불가능합니다.
That hair salon is so famous that it is impossible to make a reservation.

파마하기 전에 이 가운을 입으세요.
Let's put on this gown before getting a perm.

저는 머리를 너무 짧게 자르는 게 싫어서 그냥 다듬기만 합니다.
I don't like to get my hair cut too short, so I just get a trim.

염색하다
get one's hair died,
dye [color] one's hair

탈색하다
get one's hair bleached,
bleach one's hair

드라이하다
get one's hair blow-dried,
blow-dry one's hair

올림머리를 하다
get one's hair put up, put one's hair up

머리를 묶다
get one's hair tied, tie one's hair

헤어왁스/헤어젤로 머리를 정리하다
get one's hair fixed with hair wax / hair gel,
fix one's hair with hair wax / hair gel

머리를 펴다
get one's hair straightened,
straighten one's hair

그녀가 (직접) 탈색하고 염색하려 했을 때 머리카락 대부분이 떨어져 나갔습니다.
Most of her hair fell off when she bleached her hair and tried to dye it.

승무원들은 보통 머리를 올리고 헤어젤로 고정합니다.
Flight attendants usually put their hair up and fix it with hair gel.

마사지 복으로 갈아입다
change into
massage clothes

상의를 탈의하다
take off one's
top [shirt]

족욕을 하다
take a foot bath

전신 마사지를 받다
get [receive] a
full-body massage

몸에 오일을 바르다
apply oil to one's
body

아로마 오일 마사지를 받다
get [receive] an
aroma oil massage

발 마사지를 받다
get [receive] a foot
massage [a footrub]

경락 마사지를 받다
get [receive] a
meridian massage

두피 마사지를 받다
get [receive] a
scalp massage

등에 마사지 스톤을 올리다
put a massage stone
on one's back

긴장 풀기 위해
향을 피우다
burn incense to relax

SENTENCES TO USE

너무 부끄러워서 마사지 받으려고 상의 탈의를 못 하겠다면, 마사지샵에 가지 마세요.
If you are too shy to take off your top for a massage, please don't go to the massage parlour.

족욕을 하면서 뜨거운 차를 마시면 몸의 긴장이 굉장히 풀어집니다.
Drinking hot tea while taking a foot bath is very relaxing.

저는 베트남이나 태국을 방문할 때 아로마 오일 마사지 받는 걸 무척 좋아합니다.
I love getting aroma oil massages when I visit Vietnam or Thailand.

건식 마사지가 좋으세요? 오일 마사지가 좋으세요?　Would you like a dry massage or an oil massage?

안마사가 저를 편안하게 해주려고 향을 피웠지만, 저는 그 냄새가 싫습니다.
The masseuse burned incense to get me relaxed, but I don't like the scent of it.

3 네일케어

MP3 **088**

네일을(네일 아트를) 받다
have [get] one's nails done,
have [get] a manicure

발 관리를 받다
have [get] a
pedicure

네일 디자인을 고르다
choose nail
designs

(손톱에) 젤네일을 받다
have gel
nails applied

젤 네일을 제거하다
have gel nails removed,
remove [take off] gel nails

~에 네일 스티커를 붙이다
put nail stickers on ~

손톱/발톱을 관리받다
have one's fingernails /
toenails cared for

발의 각질을 제거하다
get the dead skin
removed from one's feet

~에 가짜 손톱을 붙이다
put fake [false]
nails on ~

내성 발톱 치료를 받다
get ingrown toenails treated,
take care of [treat] ingrown toenails

SENTENCES TO USE

고르는 걸 잘 못하는 사람에게는 네일 디자인 고르는 것도 쉬운 일이 아니에요.
Choosing a nail design isn't easy for people who have difficulty selecting.

젤 네일을 제거하는 건 시간이 오래 걸립니다.   Removing gel nails takes a long time.

대부분의 여성들이 소녀였을 때 손가락에 네일 스티커를 붙여 본 적이 있습니다.
Most women have put nail stickers on their fingers as a girl.

손톱 좀 그만 물어뜯어요! 나중에는 가짜 손톱을 붙여야 할 거예요.
Stop biting your nails! You are going to have to put fake nails on later.

요즘 많은 남자들이 네일샵에서 내성 발톱 치료를 받습니다.
A lot of men get their ingrown toenails treated at the nail salon nowadays.

피부 관리

화장을 지우다
remove one's makeup

기초화장을 하다
put on [apply] basic skin care

피부과에 가다
go to the dermatologist

얼굴 각질을 제거하다
exfoliate one's face

피부 관리법을 공유하다
share one's skincare tips [routine]

여드름을 짜다
squeeze [pop] one's pimple [acne]

SENTENCES TO USE

잠자기 전에 꼭 화장을 지우세요.
Please make sure to remove your makeup before going to bed.

매일 하는 얼굴 각질 제거를 멈추세요. 피부가 자극돼 민감해질 거예요.
Stop exfoliating your face every day, you're going to agitate your skin.

많은 뷰티 인플루언서들이 자신들의 효과적인 피부 관리 루틴을 공유합니다.
Lots of beauty influencers share their effective skincare routines.

점을 빼다
remove [take out] a mole,
have a mole removed

안면 마사지를 받다
get a facial massage

마스크팩을 하다
apply [do] a face [facial] mask

~에 얼음찜질을 하다
apply [put] an ice pack on ~

피부가 예민해지다
one's skin becomes
sensitive, agitate one's skin

~를 제모하다
wax one's ~ hair,
get ~ hair removal

선크림을 바르다
wear sun cream
[sunscreen, sunblock]

미아는 피부과에 가서 안면 마사지 받는 걸 좋아합니다.
Mia likes to get facial massages when she goes to the dermatologist.

부은 눈에 얼음찜질을 하면 부기가 가라앉을 거예요.
Putting an ice pack on your puffy eyes will decrease the swelling.

다이어트하다, 식이 요법을 하다
go [be] on a diet

체중을 감량하다
lose weight

체지방을 줄이다
lose [reduce] body fat

근육량을 늘리다
gain [increase] muscle mass

홈트레이닝을 하다
do an
at-home workout

다이어트 컨설팅을 받다
receive [get] (a) diet consulting

SENTENCES TO USE

나이가 들수록 다이어트하는 게 더 힘들어집니다.
Going on a diet gets harder as one gets older.

다이어트에서는 체지방을 줄이고 근육량을 늘리는 것이 중요합니다.
It is important to lose body fat and gain muscle mass in a diet.

엄마와 저는 매일 아침에 홈트레이닝을 합니다.
My mother and I do an at-home workout every morning.

다이어트 식단을 짜다
plan out a diet menu [meal plan]

소식하다
eat little [light], eat like a bird

닭가슴살을 많이 주문하다
order a lot of chicken breast

단백질 셰이크를 섭취하다
take [eat, drink] a protein shake

체중 변화를 체크하다
check one's weight change

다이어트 컨설턴트와 식단을 짰습니다.
I planned out a meal plan with my diet consultant.

적게 먹고 많이 움직이는 것이 살을 빼는 핵심 포인트입니다.
Eating light and moving a lot is the key point in losing weight.

단백질 셰이크를 많이 먹는다고 근육이 생기지 않습니다. 운동을 해야 한다고요!
Drinking lots of protein shakes does not give you muscle. You need to work out!

이미지 컨설팅을 받다
get [receive] image consulting

정기적으로 안면 마사지/피부 관리를 받다
get [receive] a facial / a skin treatment regularly

성형수술을 하다
get [undergo] plastic surgery

보톡스를 맞다
get a Botox (injection)

헤어 스타일링을 받다
get one's hair styled

화장하다
put on makeup

SENTENCES TO USE

저는 어머니와 함께 정기적으로 피부과에서 안면 마사지를 받습니다.
I regularly get a facial at my dermatologist with my mother.

기상캐스터는 방송하기 전에 화장을 하고 머리 스타일링을 받았습니다.
A weather forecaster put on makeup and got her hair styled before she aired.

표정 관리를 하다
control one's facial
expression

거울을 보고 표정 연습을 하다
practice one's facial expressions in the mirror

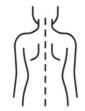

자세/체형 교정을 받다
have [get] one's posture / body corrected

퍼스널 컬러를 진단받다
get [receive] a personal color diagnosis

발성/발음 교정을 받다
have vocal
/ pronunciation
correction

대화술 관련 책을 읽다
read a book about conversation skills

크리스 씨는 늘 허리를 굽히고 있어서 자세 교정이 필요합니다.
Mr. Chris needs to get his posture corrected because he is slouching all the time.

퍼스널 컬러를 진단받고 그동안 저에게 안 어울리는 색의 옷을 입었다는 것을 알게 되었습니다.
After getting a personal color diagnosis, I found out that I've been wearing clothes that
don't look good on me.

자신감을 얻고 싶다면 대화술 관련 책을 읽어 보는 건 어때요?
Why don't you try reading a book about conversation skills if you want to gain confidence?

좋은 이미지를 위해 북미권에서 지켜야 할 에티켓

상황에 맞는 적당한 거리를 두고 대화하기

북미권 원어민과 대화할 때는 친밀도에 따라 유지해야 할 거리 기준이 암묵적으로 정해져 있습니다. 미국의 인류학자 Edward T. Hall의 연구에 따르면 상대방과의 친밀도에 따라서 네 가지로 거리를 나누는 기준이 있다고 하네요. 먼저 반경 45cm 이내의 가까운 거리에서 소통할 수 있는 가족, 애인과 같은 매우 밀접한 관계의 사람들과의 대화 공간을 intimate space라고 부릅니다. 반경 46cm~122cm 이내의 거리는 personal space라고 하여 주로 친한 친구나 신뢰할 수 있는 관계가 형성된 사람과의 대화를 위한 거리입니다. 약 1.2m~3.6m가 떨어진 거리의 대화 공간은 social space라고 부르며 보통은 알고 지내는 사람과의 대화를 위한 거리입니다. 3.7m 이상의 거리를 두는 경우는 public space라고 하여 불특정 대상과 소통할 때의 거리입니다. 즉, 북미권에서는 상대방과의 친밀한 정도에 따라 적당한 거리를 두고 대화를 나누는 것이 기본적인 에티켓인 것이죠. 줄을 설 때 너무 가까이 서 있거나, 상대방에게 가까이 접근해서 길을 묻거나, 모르는 사람에게 가벼운 터치를 하는 행동은 상대방에게 매우 무례해 보일 수 있기 때문에 주의해야 합니다.

자신감 있게 악수하기와 눈을 마주보며 대화하기

비즈니스 상황에서 첫 만남의 경우 서로를 소개하며 명함을 교환하거나 악수를 하기도 합니다. 북미권에서 만날 때 하는 악수는 firm handshake 라고 하여 상대방의 눈을 마주보고 자신감 넘치는 밝은 표정으로 오른

손을 한 번 꽉 잡고 가볍게 흔들어 주는 악수를 합니다. 이는 상대방에게 여러분의 자신감과 신뢰감을 보여주는 행동입니다. 하지만 우리나라 사람들은 악수할 때 상대방의 눈을 마주치지 않고 왼손으로 오른손목 부위를 잡고 오른손으로 상대방의 손끝 부분만을 가볍게 잡고 악수를 청할 때가 많은데, 이는 limp handshake라고 하여 서구권에서는 자신감 없고 상대방을 불편해하거나 회피하는 뉘앙스로 오해를 받을 수 있으니 주의해야 합니다. 북미권에서는 대화를 나눌 때도 상대방과 눈을 마주치면서 당당하게 소통해야 합니다. 눈 마주보는 게 부담스러워 아래를 보거나 다른 곳을 보며 이야기할 경우, 자신감이 부족해 보이거나 진정성이 없는 대화 자세로 생각해서 좋은 관계 형성이 어려워질 수 있으니 주의해야 합니다.

문 잡고 다음 사람 기다려 주기

우리나라에서는 바로 뒤에 따라오는 경우가 아니라면 뒤의 사람들을 위해 문을 붙잡고 기다려 줄 필요가 없습니다. 하지만 북미권에서는 뒤따라오는 사람이 조금 멀리 있더라도 문을 잡고 기다려 주거나 뒤따라오는 사람들이 여러 명일 때 맨 앞에서 문을 연 사람이 문을 붙잡고 나머지 사람들이 입장할 때까지 기다려 주는 것이 일반적인 매너입니다. 반대로 상대방이 문을 열고 여러분의 입장을 기다려 줄 때는 가볍게 "Thank you"라고 인사해 주세요.

I am sorry라고 말할 때는 정말 미안한 표정으로

상대방에게 사과해야 할 상황에서 "I am sorry"라고 말해야 하면, 정말 미안한 감정을 담아서 진지한 표정으로 해야 합니다. 사과를 표현할 때 표정이 무미건조하거나 웃으면서 말하면 진정성이 부족해 보이거나 비아냥조로 오해할 수 있기 때문에 주의해야 합니다.

A 제가 지금보다 더 호감 가는 상으로 보이려면 어떻게 해야 할까요?
▶ What should I do to look more likable than I am now?

B 먼저 헤어스타일을 바꾸셔야 해요.
● You have to change your hairstyle first.

반곱슬에 긴 머리는 지저분해 보이고 관리하기도 어려워요.
● Semi-curly and long hair can look messy and be hard to manage.

나이에 비해 새치도 많이 있는 편이니 짙은 갈색 계통으로 염색한 쇼트커트가 잘 어울릴 것 같아요.
● You seem to have more gray hair for your age, so I think you'll look good in a short cut with a dark brown color.

A 네, 피부 관리는 어떻게 해야 할까요?
▶ Yes, how about my skincare?

B 피부가 건조한 편이니 보습 마스크 팩을 이틀에 한 번씩 꾸준히 해 주세요.
● Since your skin is dry, make sure to use a moisturizing facial mask every other day.

얼굴에 있는 점은 다 빼고 각질도 제거해야 할 것 같아요.
● You should get your moles removed from your face and exfoliate.

얼굴에 있는 흉터도 없애야 하니 ABC 피부과에서 스킨케어 B 타입 관리를 추천합니다.
● I also recommend you to get skin care type B at ABC dermatology because you need to get scar removal.

A 알겠습니다. 체형 관리는 어떻게 하죠?
▶ Okay. How about managing my body shape?

B 몸무게가 정상 체중 대비 10kg 과체중입니다.
● You are 10kg overweight to your normal weight.

체지방은 줄이고 근육량은 늘려야 하기 때문에 유산소 운동과 웨이트 트레이닝을 병행해야 합니다.
● You need to reduce body fat and increase muscle mass, so you need to focus on aerobic exercise and weight training at the same time.

상체에 비해 하체 근육이 부실해서
하체 단련 프로그램을 진행할
거예요.
● Your lower body muscles
are weak compared to the
upper body, so we are going
to proceed with the lower
body training program.

식단이 가장 중요한데 저희가
제공해 드리는 다이어트 식단대로
드셔야 하고, 다이어트 끝날 때까지
염분이 많은 음식은 드시면
안 됩니다.
● Your diet is the most
important thing, you should
eat according to the diet we
provide and you should not
eat salty food until the end of
the diet.

A 요요가 올까 걱정이네요.
▶ I am worried about the yo-
yo effect.

B 저희 한방 다이어트 프로그램은
체력 증진에도 도움을 주기 때문에,
저희 프로그램을 계속 하면서
운동하시면 요요 현상은
걱정하지 않으셔도 될 겁니다.
● Our oriental diet program
helps improve your physical
health, so if you continue with
our program and exercise, you
won't have to worry about
that.

저희의 자세 교정 클리닉도
함께하시는 것을 추천합니다.
● I also recommend you to
join our posture correction
clinic.

A 아이고 세상에나! 비용이 많이
들 것 같은데 프로그램별로
가격 정리해서 알려 주세요.
▶ That's a lot! It seems like it
would cost a lot, so please set
up a list of the prices for each
program and let me know.

CHAPTER

12

사랑

LOVE

소개팅 & 미팅

~에게 지인을 소개하다
introduce one's
acquaintance to ~

소개팅을 주선하다
set [fix] up on
a blind date

소개팅을 하다
go on a blind date

단체 미팅을 하다
have a group meeting [date]

번개팅에 나가다
go speed dating [date]

취미 생활을 공유하다
share one's hobby

공통의 관심사를 이야기하다
share [talk about] a common interest

SENTENCES TO USE

내가 소개팅시켜 준 커플들은 다 결혼에 성공했습니다.
All the couples I set up on a blind date succeeded in getting married.

대학 다닐 때 친구들과 번개팅에 나가는 건 재미있습니다.
It's fun to go speed dating with friends in college.

로완은 데이트 상대랑 공통된 관심사와 취미를 공유한 후 다음 데이트를 계획했습니다.
Rowan planned for the next date after he and his date shared common interests and hobbies.

MP3 093

정중히 거절하다
decline [end]
politely
[respectfully]

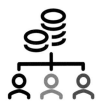

각자 계산하다
pay one's bills separately, go Dutch,
split the check [bill]

식사 후 디저트를 먹다
have a dessert
after a meal

주선자에게 연락해서 화내다
call the middleman
[go-between] and get angry

인연이 아니다
be not meant to be, be not
destined for each other

~에게 애프터 신청을 하다
ask ~ on [for]
a second date

애프터 신청을 거절하다
refuse to go on a second date,
turn down [decline] a second date

데이트 상대가 마음에 들지 않으면, 무례하게 굴지 말고 정중히 거절하세요.
If you don't like your date, please don't be rude and decline respectfully.

그 사람이 저에게 더 이상 문자를 하지 않아요. 우린 인연이 아니었나 봅니다.
He stopped texting me. I guess we weren't meant to be.

첫눈에 반하다
be in love at
first sight

사랑에 눈이 멀다(콩깍지가 씌다)
be blinded by love, fall head over heels

데이트하다
go on a date

~에게 마음이 있다
have a thing [a feeling] for ~

썸을 타다
have a fling

밀당하다
play hard to get,
play games

(~와) 더블데이트를 하다
go on a double date (with),
double-date (with)

SENTENCES TO USE

첫눈에 반한 사랑은 아니었지만, 그는 결국 사랑에 눈이 멀었습니다.
It was not love at first sight, but he was eventually blinded by love.

전 밀당을 하기에는 나이가 좀 있으니, 제가 마음에 드신다면 그냥 말씀해 주세요.
I am a little old to play hard to get, so if you like me, please just tell me.

그 커플은 더블데이트를 했고, 결국 상대 커플의 파트너들과 사랑에 빠져 버렸습니다.
That couple went on a double date, and ended up falling in love with the other couple's
partners.

고백하다
confess one's feelings [love],
ask someone out

(~와) 사귀다, 연애하다
go out (with), have a (romantic)
relationship (with)

연애편지를 쓰다
write a love letter

다음 데이트 약속을 잡다
set [plan for] a next date

마음을 담아 꽃을 선물하다
present [give] flowers with all one's heart

온라인 데이트를 하다
date online

트로이는 데이트 앱에서 만난 여자와 사귀기 시작했습니다.
Troy started going out with the girl he met on a dating app.

우리가 썸탈 때 그는 나에게 연애편지를 쓰고 선물을 주곤 했습니다.
He used to write me love letters and give me gifts when we were having a fling.

MP3 095

프러포즈 이벤트를 준비하다
arrange [prepare] a
proposal event

약혼반지를 준비하다
prepare an
engagement ring

프러포즈 장소를 예약하다
reserve a place for
one's proposal

친구들에게 도움을 청하다
ask one's friends
for help

(전화해서) 연인을 부르다
call in one's
lover

아무 일 없는 듯 연기하다
act as if nothing had
happened, play innocent

로맨틱한 분위기를 만들다
create a romantic
atmosphere

연인에게 청혼하다
propose to
one's lover

청혼에 성공하다
succeed in
proposing

연인과 키스하다
kiss one's
lover

(결혼) 프러포즈를 거절하다
turn down one's
(marriage) proposal

실패의 충격에 당황하다
be embarrassed by
the shock of failure

SENTENCES TO USE

그는 모든 행사를 준비하고 나서 프러포즈할 장소 예약하는 것을 잊었습니다.
He arranged a whole event and then forgot to reserve a place for his proposal.

혼자 할 수 없을 것 같으면, 친구들에게 도움을 요청해 보세요.
If you don't think you can do it yourself, ask your friends for help.

로맨틱한 분위기를 만들고 아무 일 없는 듯 연기하는 것이 프러포즈 성공의 비결입니다.
Creating a romantic atmosphere and playing innocent is a key to success in proposing.

케이티는 남자 친구가 그녀의 청혼을 승낙한 후 남자 친구에게 키스를 했습니다.
Katie kissed her boyfriend after he said yes to her proposal.

다이애나가 랠프의 프러포즈를 거절하리라고 누가 생각이나 했겠어요?
Who would have thought that Diana would turn down Ralph's proposal?

4 다툼 & 이별

MP3 096

사랑싸움을 하다
have a lover's
quarrel

(헤어지고 나서)
다시 만나다, 재결합하다
get back together

~와 바람을 피우다
cheat on ~, have an affair with ~,
play [fool] around with ~

바람 피우다 걸리다
be [get] caught
cheating

서운함(실망감)을 표현하다
express one's
disappointment

~와 헤어지다
break [split]
up with ~

~을 차다
dump ~,
drop ~

차이다
be [get] dumped
[dropped]

전화번호를
차단하다
block one's
phone number

함께 찍은 사진들을
삭제하다
delete the pictures
taken together

추억을 간직하다
keep [cherish,
treasure] one's
memory

파혼하다
break off one's
engagement
[wedding]

이혼하다
get divorced,
get a divorce

SENTENCES TO USE

많은 커플들이 터놓고 이야기를 나눈 후에는 다시 만납니다.
Many couples get back together after talking things out.

멜리사는 사랑싸움 후에 실망감을 표현했습니다.
Melissa expressed her disappointment after a lover's quarrel.

제가 그를 차 버린 건 알지만, 그래도 여전히 우리의 추억은 소중히 여겨요!
I know I dumped him, but I still cherish our memories!

해리는 전 여자 친구와 바람을 피우다 걸린 후 차였습니다.
Harry got dumped after he was caught cheating with his ex-girlfriend.

저는 헤어진 후에는 늘 전 남자 친구의 전화번호를 차단합니다.
I always block my ex-boyfriend's phone number after I split up.

MP3 097

상견례를 하다
have [arrange] a meeting between the families of the couple to be wed

신랑/신붓집에 방문하다
visit the groom's / bride's house

결혼 승낙을 받다
ask one's permission [blessing] for marriage, ask for the hand of ~

웨딩 플래너와 상담하다
consult a wedding planner

예식장을 계약하다
make a contract with a wedding hall [venue]

결혼사진을 촬영하다
take one's wedding photos

웨딩드레스/턱시도를 입어 보다
try on a wedding dress / a tuxedo

웨딩드레스/턱시도를 빌리다
rent a wedding dress / a tuxedo

신혼여행지를 정하다
choose [decide on] a honeymoon destination

청첩장을 돌리다
send [give] out wedding invitations

신부 화장을 받다
receive [get] bridal makeup

SENTENCES TO USE

그는 부모님께 결혼 승낙을 받으러 그녀의 집에 갔습니다.
He went to her house to ask her parents' permission for their marriage.

웨딩 플래너를 통해 예식장을 계약하면 시간과 돈을 절약할 수 있습니다.
Making a wedding hall contract through a wedding planner can save time and money.

그녀는 결혼 사진 찍을 때 입을 아름다운 드레스를 빌리려고 혹독한 다이어트를 하고 있었습니다.
She was on a harsh diet to rent a beautiful dress for her wedding photos.

많은 연인들이 신혼여행지를 정하려고 할 때 다툽니다.
A lot of couples fight when they are trying to decide on a honeymoon destination.

청첩장을 나눠 주는 친구를 만나는 것은 항상 놀라운 일입니다.
It's always surprising to meet a friend when they are giving out wedding invitations.

결혼하다
get married, settle down,
tie the knot, get hitched

축의금을 내다
pay [give]
congratulatory
money

스몰 웨딩을 하다
have a small
[garden, house]
wedding

전통 혼례를 하다
have a traditional
wedding

주례사를 듣다
listen to the
officiating speech

부케를 던지다
throw
a bouquet

결혼식 사회를 보다
host a wedding
ceremony

결혼식에서 축가를 부르다
sing at [for]
a wedding

혼인 서약을 하다
exchange wedding
[marriage] vows

하객들과 사진을 찍다
take pictures with
the guests

피로연에 참석하다
attend [go to]
a reception

신혼여행을 떠나다
go on
a honeymoon

SENTENCES TO USE

요즘은 스몰 웨딩을 올리고 호화로운 신혼여행을 가는 것이 유행입니다.
Having a small wedding and going on a luxury honeymoon is a trend nowadays.

전통 혼례식을 빼 버리면 결혼식 예산을 절약할 수 있습니다.
You can save on wedding budget by taking out the traditional wedding ceremony.

우리 언니 결혼식에서 유명 가수가 축가를 불렀습니다.
A famous singer sang at my sister's wedding.

주례사 없이 혼인서약만 하고 결혼식을 간결하게 하도록 해요.
Let's keep the wedding concise by exchanging wedding vows without the officiating speech.

커플들은 보통 피로연이 끝난 후에 신혼여행을 갑니다.
A couple usually goes on their honeymoon after the reception ends.

A 자기야, 상견례도 끝나고 결혼 날짜도 잡혔으니까 이제 결혼식 준비를 하나씩 해 보자.
▶ Babe, since we met each other's parents and decided on a date, let's start planning for our wedding.

친구가 웨딩 플래너를 통해서 준비했는데 다 마음에 들었다고 해.
▶ My friend prepared everything through a wedding planner and loved everything about it.

B 얼마 전에 결혼한 해나 씨 말이야?
● You mean Hannah who got married recently?

결혼사진도 예쁘게 나오고 웨딩드레스랑 메이크업도 세련되고 예쁘던데.
● Her wedding photos came out pretty, the wedding dress and the makeup were stylish and pretty as well.

우리도 그 플래너에게 상담받아 볼까?
● Should we consult with her planner too?

A 좋아. 예식장은 어떻게 할까?
▶ Good. What about the wedding venue?

가성비 좋은 일반 웨딩홀부터 고급호텔 예식홀까지 가격 차이가 천차만별이더라고.
▶ The price difference is huge from cost-effective regular venues to luxury hotel venues.

B 전에 이야기했던 것처럼 가족이랑 친한 친구들만 불러서 스몰 웨딩 하는 것은 어때? 지난번에 내 다른 절친이 몬트그린 베이에 있는 펜션에서 결혼했잖아. 나는 그런 식으로 적은 인원만 불러서 파티하면서 결혼식하면 좋겠어.
● How about having a small wedding with family and close friends like we talked before? My other best friend got married at a pension in Montgreen Bay. I want to only invite a small number of people like that and have a wedding with a party.

A 그래. 스몰 웨딩도 고려해 보자.
▶ Okay, let's take small weddings into consideration.

신혼여행은 어디로 갈지 생각해 봤어?
▶ Have you thought about the honeymoon destination?

B 난 몰디브가 제일 좋을 것 같아.
● I think the Maldives is the best.

일주일 정도 바닷가에서 수영하고 마사지 받으면 좋을 것 같은데.
● It would be nice to go swimming and get massages at the beach for about a week.

자기는 어때?
● How about you?

A 음… 사실 난 유럽 같은 데 가서 여기저기 관광 다니고 맛있는 것 먹고 멋진 야경도 보고 다양한 활동을 해보고 싶은데.
▶ Hmm… Actually, I want to go to places like Europe and go sightseeing, eat delicious food, see the great night view, and do various activities.

B 난 신혼여행은 누구 간섭받지 않고 우리 둘만의 시간을 보내는 게 좋은데.
● I want our honeymoon to be just the two of us without other people's interference.

자기는 그렇지 않아?
● Don't you think so?

A 바다 보고 마사지만 받기에는 몰디브가 거리도 멀고 좀 비싼 것 같아.
▶ The Maldives seems to be a little expensive and far away for beach massages.

좀 더 가깝고 저렴한 곳을 찾아보는 건 어때?
▶ Why don't we look for a place that is closer and more affordable?

B 그러면 좀 더 생각해 보자.
● Then, let's give it some more thought.

마침 다음 달에 웨딩 박람회가 있으니까 거기 가서 상담받아 보는 건 어때?
● There is a wedding fair next month, so why don't we get a consultation over there?

A 그게 좋겠네!
▶ That'd be great!

박람회에서 상담받고 견적 받아 본 거랑 웨딩 플래너 견적서랑 비교해 보고 결정하면 좋을 것 같아.
▶ It would be good to decide after comparing wedding fair consultation and estimates by the wedding planner.

13

행사

EVENTS

이벤트를 기획하다
organize [plan] an event

파티룸을 예약하다
reserve a party room

부케를/케이크를/선물을 준비하다
prepare a bouquet / a cake / a gift

깜짝 이벤트를 하다
have [hold] a surprise
event [party]

파티에 ~를 초대하다
invite ~ to
the party

파티에 참석하다
attend
a party

출장 뷔페를 부르다
hire a buffet caterer,
call a caterer

짧은 영상을 준비하다
prepare
a short video

기념일/생일을 축하하다
celebrate one's
anniversary / birthday

기념사진을 찍다
take a commemorative
photo

~로 건배하다
make a toast
with ~

SENTENCES TO USE

그는 결혼기념일을 위해 부케와 다이아몬드 반지를 준비했습니다.
He prepared a bouquet and a diamond ring for his wedding anniversary.

우와! 루시아가 생일 파티에 유명 인플루언서들을 초대했어!
Wow! Lucia invited famous influencers to her birthday party!

파티 플래너는 호텔 출장 뷔페를 부르는 데 예산 대부분을 썼습니다.
The party planner spent most of the budget on hiring a hotel buffet caterer.

제가 파티에서 보여주고 싶은 짧은 축하 영상을 준비했습니다.
I prepared a short congratulatory video that I want to show at the party.

이 사랑스러운 커플을 위해 샴페인 잔으로 건배해요!
Let's make a toast with our champagne glasses for this lovely couple!

돌잔치를 하다
have one's first
birthday party

금반지를 선물하다
give a gold ring
as a present

아기 성장 동영상을 시청하다
watch a baby's
growth video

돌잡이를 하다
do a doljabi

답례품을 돌리다/받다
give out / receive
a return gift

성년식을 하다
hold a coming-of-age
ceremony

환갑/칠순/팔순을 축하하다
celebrate one's 60th /
70th / 80th birthday

가족을/친구를 초대하다
invite one's
family / friends

밤새 춤추고 즐기다
dance and enjoy
all night

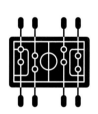

파티 게임을 하고 놀다
play party games

사람들과 어울려 놀다
hang out [socialize]
with people

SENTENCES TO USE

저는 (여자) 조카 돌잔치 때 금반지를 선물로 주었습니다.
I gave a gold ring as a present for my niece at her first birthday party.

수건처럼 뻔한 선물이 아닌 독특한 답례품을 주는 게 어때요?
Why don't you give out unique return gifts not boring gifts like towels?

제이미는 작년에 성년식을 했습니다.
Jamie held her coming-of-age ceremony last year.

아버지는 할머니 팔순 축하를 위해 인기 트로트 가수를 불렀습니다.
My father hired a popular trot singer for my grandmother's 80th birthday celebration.

저는 20대 때 친구들과 밤새도록 파티 게임을 하고 춤을 추곤 했습니다.
I used to play party games and dance all night with my friends during my 20s.

생일 파티에 초대하다
invite to one's birthday party

생일 선물을 주다
give a birthday present

파티 참석 여부를 회답해 주다
RSVP to a party,
reply one's attendance
of a party

케이크를 주문 제작하다
customize a cake,
custom-make a cake

케이크에 초를 꽂다
put [stick] candles on a cake

초에 불을 붙이다
light a candle

SENTENCES TO USE

어머나! 이번 주 토요일에 있을 그의 파티에 참석 여부 회답해 주는 것을 깜빡했어요.
Oops! I forgot to RSVP to his party this Saturday.

(여자) 조카가 자기 생일에 유니콘 모양의 주문 제작 케이크를 원했습니다.
My niece wanted a custom-made unicorn shaped cake for her birthday.

생일 축하 노래를 부르다
sing a 'Happy Birthday' song

촛불을 불어서 끄다
blow out
a candle

장난으로 얼굴에 생크림을 묻히다
put whipped cream on
one's face for fun

샴페인을 터트리다
pop the champagne

생일 파티를 즐기다
enjoy one's birthday party

촛불 켜고 나서 '생일 축하' 노래를 부르도록 해요.
Let's sing a 'Happy Birthday' song after lighting the candles.

장난으로 생크림을 얼굴에 묻혔다고 루나가 화를 냈다니 믿기지 않아요!
I can't believe Luna got mad for putting whipped cream on her face for fun!

나는 어제 일은 잊고 내일 있을 토니의 생일 파티를 즐길 거예요.
I am going to forget what happened yesterday and enjoy Tony's birthday party tomorrow.

임종을 지켜보다
watch over one's passing
[death]

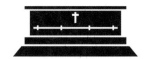

장례식장을 계약하다
make [sign] a contract with
a funeral home

장지를 정하다
decide on a burial
ground

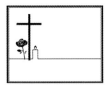

부고장을 작성하다
write an obituary
notice

부고 메시지를 보내다
send an obituary
message

부고 기사를 올리다
publish an
obituary

영정 사진을 준비하다
prepare a portrait
of the deceased

빈소를 마련하다
set up a mortuary
[a funeral parlor]

상복을 준비하다
prepare mourning
(clothes)

조문객을 위한 음식을 준비하다
prepare food for condolers
[mourners]

SENTENCES TO USE

많은 사람들이 사랑하는 이의 임종을 지켜본 후에 트라우마를 느낍니다.
Many people get traumatized after watching over their loved one's passing.

장례식장 계약이 누가 돌아가신 후에 가장 먼저 해야 할 일입니다.
Signing a contract with a funeral home is the first thing one should do after someone passes.

부고장 좀 대신 써 주시겠어요? 제가 빈소 준비하느라 바빠서요.
Could you write an obituary notice for me? I am busy setting up the funeral parlor.

예전엔 사람들이 신문에 부고 기사를 내곤 했습니다.
People used to publish an obituary on newspapers.

이런, 상복 준비할 시간이 없어요.
Oh no, I don't have time to prepare mourning.

4 장례식 진행

MP3 103

상복을 입다
wear mourning
(clothes)

조문객을 받다
accept [welcome]
condolers [mourners]

제사를 지내다
hold a memorial
service [ceremony]

분향하다
burn [offer]
incense

고인에게 헌화하다
lay flowers for the
deceased

입관식을 하다
hold a coffin rite
ceremony

화장장으로/장지로 이동하다
move [go] to the
crematorium / burial site

고인의 유지대로 화장하다
cremate as the will
[wish] of the deceased

유골을 납골당에 안치하다
place one's remains [ashes]
in the charnel house

유골을 뿌리다
scatter one's
remains [ashes]

고인을 매장하다
bury the
deceased

SENTENCES TO USE

제사 때 향을 피우는 것이 일반적입니다.
It is normal to burn incense at the memorial service.

저희 집에는 고인에게 헌화하는 전통이 있습니다.
There is a tradition of laying flowers for the deceased in my family.

우리 같이 장지에 가서 고인을 묻어 드리자고요.
Let's go to the burial site together and bury the deceased.

그녀의 유골은 납골당에 안치되어 있습니다.
Her remains are placed in the charnel house.

제인은 아버지가 원한 대로 아버지의 유골을 해변에 뿌려 드렸습니다.
Jane scattered her father's ashes at the beach as he wished.

부고 메시지를 받다
receive an obituary message

위로의 메시지를 보내다
send a message of consolation

빈소에 화환을 보내다
send a wreath to the mortuary

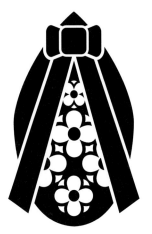

검정색 타이를 매다
wear a black tie

검정색 정장을 입다
wear a black suit

장례식장에 가다
go to [visit] a funeral home

SENTENCES TO USE

저는 친구한테서 부고 메시지를 받자마자 빈소에 화환을 보냈습니다.
I sent a wreath to the mortuary as soon as I received an obituary message from a friend.

남자들은 보통 검정색 양복에 검정 넥타이를 매고 장례식장에 갑니다.
Men usually wear a black suit and a tie to a funeral home.

장례식장에 가야 해서 오늘 약속을 취소해야 해요.
I need to cancel our appointment today because I need to go to a funeral home.

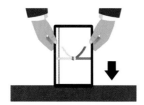

조의금을 내다
pay [give] condolence money

(영정 사진에) 묵념을 올리다
pay [offer] a silent prayer [tribute]
(to the portrait of the deceased)

고인을 애도하다
mourn for the deceased

장례식장에서 식사를 하다
dine at a funeral home

유가족을 위로하다
comfort one's bereaved family

사람들은 보통 조의금으로 얼마를 내나요?
How much do people usually give for condolence money?

묵념하고 유가족을 위로하러 갑시다.
Let's pay a silent tribute and go comfort the bereaved.

A　삼가 고인의 명복을 빕니다.
▶ I am sorry for your loss.

B　이렇게 먼 곳까지 찾아와 조문해
주셔서 감사합니다.
● Thank you for coming all
this way to pay your respects.

A　어르신께서 얼마 전까지 건강하신
줄 알았는데 갑자기 어떻게 되신
건가요?
▶ I thought he was healthy
until recently, what happened
all of a sudden?

B　연세가 있다 보니 자주 잔병치레를
하셨는데 갑자기 폐렴이 악화되어
별세하시게 됐습니다.
● He has been getting sick
frequently due to his age, but
his pneumonia suddenly got
worse before his passing.

그래도 가족들 다 모였을 때
유언도 남기시고 임종도 함께할 수
있어서 다행입니다.
● Still, I was glad that he was
able to leave his will and pass
on with all his family by his
side.

A　어르신께서 올해 91세셨지요?
▶ He was 91 this year, right?

가족과 함께해서 편안하게 가실 수
있으셨을 겁니다.
▶ I'm sure he was able to
move on comfortably with his
family by his side.

장지는 정해졌나요?
▶ Have you decided on a
burial site?

B　네, 삼일장이라 모레까지 조문객을
맞이하고 그다음 날에 화장장에
갈 예정입니다.
● Yes, it's a 3-day funeral so
we will accept condolers until
the day after tomorrow and go
to the crematorium.

화장 후에 유골함은 추모공원의
봉안당에 안치될 예정입니다.
● The remains will be placed
in the burial chamber in the
memorial park after cremation.

B 부모님께서 빈소에 화환도
보내주시고 조의금까지 따로
챙겨 주시니 감사할 따름입니다.
● I am so grateful for their
wreath sent to the mortuary
and condolence money.

A 그렇군요. 상심이 크실 텐데
잘 보내 드리시기 바랍니다.
▶ I see. I'm sure you are
grieving. I hope you can send
him well.

어르신께 인사 드리셨으니
저쪽에 있는 식당에서
저녁 식사하시고 가시지요.
● Since you offered your
prayers, please go to the diner
and have dinner.

저희 부모님도 함께 오시려고
했는데 몸이 불편하셔서
제가 조의금을 따로 받아왔습니다.
▶ My parents wanted to come
with me, but they weren't
feeling well so I brought their
condolence money as well.

A 네, 그렇게 하겠습니다. 감사합니다.
▶ Yes, I will do so. Thank you
very much.

CHAPTER

14

귀가 후

AFTER COMING BACK HOME

귀가

우편함을 확인하다
check one's mailbox

엘리베이터 층 버튼을 누르다
press a floor button on the elevator

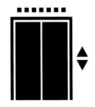

엘리베이터를 타고 올라가다
take the elevator up

집으로 돌아오다
return home, come
[get] back home

도어락 비밀번호를 입력하다
enter the door lock password

SENTENCES TO USE

저는 엘리베이터 타기 전에 항상 우편함을 확인합니다.
I always check my mailbox before getting on the elevator.

엘리베이터에서 층 버튼 누르는 걸 깜빡해서 아직 1층에 있어요!
I'm still on the first floor because I forgot to press my floor button on the elevator!

아무도 못 보게 도어락 비밀번호를 입력할 때는 손을 가리세요.
Please cover your hand when you enter the door lock password so no one can see.

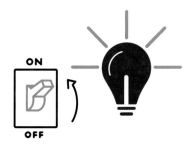

집 안의 전등을 켜다
turn on the lights in the house

가방을 내려놓다
put down one's bag, set one's bag down

옷을 벗어서 세탁기에 넣다
take off one's clothes and put them
in the washing machine

실내복으로 갈아입다
change into indoor clothes

실내용 슬리퍼를 신다
wear indoor slippers

저는 어두운 게 싫어서 집에 오면 집 안의 불을 다 켭니다.
I turn on all the lights in the house when I get home because I don't like the dark.

이웃의 층간 소음 민원 방지를 위해 실내용 슬리퍼를 신어야 합니다.
You should wear indoor slippers to prevent noise complaints from neighbors.

2 저녁 식사

냉장고에서 식재료를 꺼내다
take the ingredients out of [from]
the refrigerator

과일을/채소를 물에 씻다(헹구다)
rinse fruits / vegetables
in water

프라이팬에 고기를/생선을 굽다
grill meat / fish
in a frying pan

에어프라이어로 요리하다
cook in an air fryer,
use an air fryer to cook

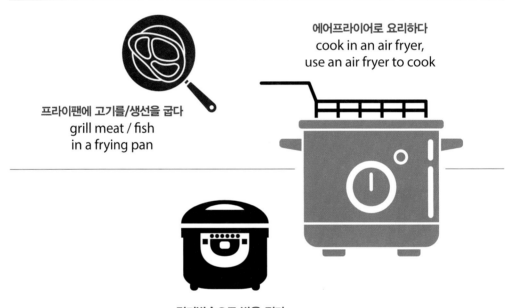

전기밥솥으로 밥을 짓다
use a rice cooker to cook rice

SENTENCES TO USE

냉장고에서 샐러드 재료 꺼내서 물에 헹궈 줄래요?
Can you take out the ingredients for salad from the refrigerator and rinse them in water?

에어프라이어를 사용해 요리하기 시작하면서 저녁 식사 준비가 더 쉬워졌습니다.
Preparing dinner became easier since I started to use an air fryer to cook.

요즘은 밥을 지을 때 밥솥을 사용하지만, 우리 할머니는 일반 냄비에 밥을 짓곤 했습니다.
We use a rice cooker to cook rice now, but my grandmother used to cook rice in regular pots.

요리를 만들다
make a dish

냉동식품을 해동하다
thaw frozen food

저녁 식사를 하다
have [eat] dinner

두 그릇을 먹다
have [eat] a second helping

배달 음식을 주문하다
order food by delivery

야식을 먹다
take [have] a late-night snack [meal]

에린은 요리하기 싫어서 중국 음식을 배달시켰습니다.
Erin ordered Chinese food by delivery because she didn't want to cook.

우리는 어제 야식으로 스파게티를 먹었습니다.
We had spaghetti for a late-night snack yesterday.

A 자기야, 오늘 많이 바빴어?
▶ Hey, honey. Were you busy today?

B 응, 아침에 거래처 갔다가 회사 복귀해서 보고서 쓰고 내일 있을 사업 설명회 발표도 준비해야 하다 보니 야근을 안 할 수가 없더라고.
● Yup, I went to a client in the morning, returned to work, wrote a report and had to prepare for tomorrow's business briefing. So, I couldn't help but work overtime.

자기는 어땠어?
● How was your day?

A 오늘 매장에 손님이 너무 많이 몰려와서 정신이 하나도 없었어.
▶ I was so busy because there were so many customers at the store today.

직원들이 다 손님 응대하고 급하게 비번인 아르바이트생한테까지 연락해서 도와달라고 했는데도 일손이 부족했어.
▶ All the employees responded to the guests and urgently contacted the off-duty part-timer for help, but we were still short-handed.

손님들이 상황을 배려해 기다려 줘서 다행이지 하마터면 항의 많이 받을 뻔했어.
▶ I was glad that the customers were considerate enough to wait, or else I would have gotten a lot of complaints.

B 자기가 일 처리를 잘하니까 아무 문제 없이 잘 돌아간 거지.
● It went well without problems because you did a great job.

사장님이 자기한테 보너스 좀 줘야 하는 거 아냐?
● Shouldn't your boss give you a bonus?

A 흐흐, 그러면 좋겠는데 우리 사장님이 내가 이렇게 고생하는 걸 아시기는 하는지 모르겠네.
▶ Ha. I hope so, but I don't know if my boss knows that I'm going through a hard time like this.

우리 이번 주말에는 뭐할까?
▶ What shall we do this weekend?

B 오랜만에 경치 좋은 곳으로 캠핑 가서 멍 때리고 힐링하고 오는 건 어때?

● Why don't we go camping in a beautiful place, zone out and have some down time since it's been a while?

A 그것도 좋긴 한데, 재미있는 영화가 개봉 많이 했으니까 영화관 가서 영화 보고 외식하는 건 어때?

▶ That's good too, but since there are a lot of interesting movies released, how about going to the movies and eating out?

몸이 너무 힘드니까 캠핑하러 가서 텐트 치고 야외에서 숙박하는 것도 부담이 되네.

▶ It's going to be a burden to go camping, set up a tent, and stay outdoors because my body is so tired.

B 좋아. 그렇게 하자.

● Okay, let's do that.

아! 이번 주 토요일에 야구 경기도 있으니까 조조 영화 보고 맛있는 점심 먹고 드라이브 좀 하다가 야구장 가서 치맥 당기면 되겠네.

● Ah! There is a baseball game this Saturday, so we can watch a movie early in the morning, have a good lunch, go for a drive, go to the game and have chicken and beer.

A 아주 좋은 생각이야.

▶ That seems like a lovely idea.

야구 경기 끝나면 공원에서 산책 좀 하다가 집에 가자.

▶ After the baseball game, let's take a walk in the park and go home.

B 콜! 이번 주 토요일은 그렇게 돌아다니고 일요일은 집에서 푹 쉬는 걸로 해.

● Great! Let's hang out like that on Saturday and rest at home on Sunday.

MP3 109

TV를 켜다
turn on
the TV

채널을 돌리다
change TV
channels

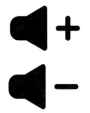

소리를 키우다/줄이다
turn up / down
the volume

TV 편성표를 대강 살펴보다
look [skim, run] through the TV
schedule [program listings]

뉴스/드라마/광고를 보다
watch the news /
dramas / commercials

프로그램의 재방송을 보다
watch a rerun
of a program

**케이블 TV로
영화를 보다**
watch a movie on
cable TV

유료 채널을 보다
watch a pay-per-view
channel

VOD/OTT 서비스를 구독하다
subscribe to VOD (Video-on-Demand) /
an OTT (Over-the-Top) media service

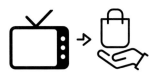

홈쇼핑 방송에서 상품을 구매하다
buy goods on a home
shopping channel

자막을 켜다
turn on the
caption [subtitle]

SENTENCES TO USE

그 퀴즈 프로그램 언제 하는지 잊어버렸는데, TV 편성표 좀 봐 줄래요?
I forgot when the game show is on, can you skim through the TV schedule for me?

저는 보통 태블릿으로는 드라마를 보고 TV로는 뉴스를 봅니다.
I usually watch dramas on my tablet and watch the news on TV.

그 드라마 안 봤으면 재방송을 꼭 보셔야 해요.
You definitely have to watch the rerun of that drama if you have not seen it.

요즘엔 사람들이 유료 채널을 보기보다는 OTT 서비스를 구독합니다.
People nowadays subscribe to an OTT media service rather than watching a pay-per-view channel.

케이블 TV로 영화를 볼 때 자막을 켜는 것이 일반적입니다.
It's typical to turn on the caption when watching a movie on cable TV.

4 컴퓨터 & 인터넷

MP3 **110**

컴퓨터를 켜다
turn on the
computer

사용자 ID와 비밀번호로 로그인하다
use one's user ID and
password to log in

웹사이트에
로그인/로그아웃하다
log in to / out of
a website

마우스를 움직여 클릭하다
move the mouse
to click

키보드로 글을 쓰다
write [type] on a keyboard

포털 사이트에 ~를 검색해 보다
search (for) ~
on a portal site

인터넷 서핑을 하다
surf [browse] the Internet

와이파이에 연결하다
connect to a Wi-Fi

이메일을 쓰다/보내다
write / send an email

이메일에 답장하다
reply to an email

SENTENCES TO USE

로그인 사용자 ID와 비밀번호를 기억할 수 없다면 어딘가에 적어 두세요.
If you can't remember your user ID and password to log in, write it down somewhere.

쇼핑 가기 전에 온라인에서 최신 트렌드를 검색해 보는 것이 좋을 거야.
You better search current trends online before you go shopping.

이 터널에서는 와이파이 연결하기가 왜 그렇게 어렵죠?
Why is it so hard to connect to a Wi-Fi in this tunnel?

와이파이 연결이 어려워서 인터넷 서핑에 컴퓨터를 사용하지 않습니다.
I don't use my computer for surfing the Internet because it is difficult to connect to a Wi-Fi.

저희가 보낸 이메일 확인하시고 최대한 빨리 회신해 주시겠어요?
Could you check the email we sent you and reply to it as soon as possible?

MP3 **111**

패턴을 입력해
스마트폰 잠금을 풀다
enter a pattern
to unlock one's phone

전화를 걸다/받다
make / take a
phone call

통화하다
talk on one's phone

영상 통화하다
make a video call

이모티콘을 사용해
문자 메시지를 보내다
send a text message
using emojis [emoticons]

사진/동영상을 보내다
send a photo /
a video

스마트폰을
업데이트하다/백업하다
update / back up
one's phone

스마트폰 설정을 변경하다
change the settings
on one's phone

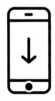

앱을 다운받아 사용하다
download and use an
application [app]

블루투스를 연결하다
connect to the
Bluetooth

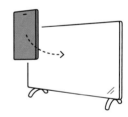

핸드폰 화면을 TV 화면에 미러링하다
mirror one's cell phone screen
to a TV screen

SENTENCES TO USE

휴대폰 잠금 해제 패턴을 잊어버릴 경우를 대비해 지문 잠금 해제도 설정해 놓으세요. Set up your fingerprint to unlock your phone just in case you forget the pattern to unlock your phone.

그녀는 남자 친구에게 보내는 문자 메시지에 하트 이모티콘을 많이 쓰곤 했습니다.
She used to send a lot of heart emojis in her text messages to her boyfriend.

이런, 핸드폰이 고장 났는데 백업을 안 한 것 같아요! Oh no, my phone broke and I don't think I backed it up!

수업 중에 울리지 않도록 휴대전화를 끄거나 설정을 변경해 주세요.
Please turn off your phones or change the settings on your phone so that it does not ring during the class.

더 큰 화면을 원하면 휴대폰 화면을 TV 화면에 미러링하는 건 어때요?
Why don't you mirror your cell phone screen to the TV screen if you want a bigger screen?

238

6 게임

게임에 접속하다
access [connect to]
a game

PC 게임/온라인 게임을 하다
play a PC game /
an online game

미션 완료 보상을 받다
be rewarded for
completing the mission

이벤트에 참여하다
participate [take part]
in an event

캐릭터를 만들다
make [create]
a character

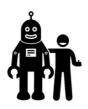

아이템을 획득하다
obtain an item

new item!

아이템들을 현질하여
(현금으로) 구매하다
buy items with real cash,
pay for items in cash

LV.99

~을 레벨업하다
level up ~

RANK

랭킹을 확인하다
check one's
ranking

~와의 대결이 시작되다
a matchup begins
[starts] with ~

연맹/클랜에 가입하다
join a league /
a clan [party]

다른 참가자와 게임을 하다
play games with
other players

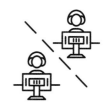

다른 참가자와 채팅을 하다
chat with
other players

SENTENCES TO USE

저는 크리스마스 이벤트 동안 미션을 완료해서 보상을 받았습니다.
I was rewarded for completing the mission during the Christmas event.

와! 다른 게임 참가자와 함께 급습할 때 희귀 아이템을 얻었어요!
Wow! I obtained a rare item when I participated in a raid with other players!

부모님 몰래 현금으로 아이템을 구매해서 곤란하게 되는 아이들이 많습니다.   There are a lot of kids who get in trouble buying items with cash behind their parent's back.

일주일 후에 클랜 대결(클랜 간 대결)이 시작됩니다.   A clan matchup will begin in a week.

원활한 게임 흐름을 경험하기 위해서는 연맹 가입을 추천합니다.
In order to experience a smooth flow of the game, we recommend joining a league.

SNS 개인 계정을 만들다
create [make]
one's SNS account

~의 SNS 채널을 구독하다
subscribe to [follow]
one's SNS channel

게시물을 훑어보다
look through
one's posts

콘텐츠에 '좋아요'를 누르다
click 'like' on the
content

~에 댓글을 달다
post [write] a
comment on ~

~에 악플을 달다
post [write] hateful
comments on ~

게시물을 공유하다
share one's post

SNS 계정에 게시물을 올리다
upload a post
on one's SNS

DM을 보내다/받다
send / get a DM
(direct message)

~의 계정을 차단하다
block one's
account

SNS에서 이벤트에
참여하다
participate in
an event on SNS

SNS에 협찬 제품을 올리다
post [upload]
sponsored products
on one's SNS

SENTENCES TO USE

저는 5년 전에 SNS 계정을 만들었고, 지금은 팔로워가 많은 인플루언서입니다.
I created my SNS account 5 years ago, and now I am an influencer with lots of followers.

제 아이들 SNS를 구독할 때마다 걔네 계정에서 차단당해요.
Every time I subscribe to my children's SNS, I get blocked from their accounts.

저는 시간이 날 때 제 친구의 SNS를 훑어보고 댓글을 남깁니다.
I look through my friend's SNS and write comments in my free time.

제나는 모르는 사람으로부터 부적절한 DM을 많이 받습니다.
Jenna gets inappropriate DMs from strangers a lot.

유명 인플루언서들은 SNS에 협찬 제품들을 올려서 많은 돈을 받습니다.
Famous influencers get paid a lot for uploading sponsored products on their SNS.

8 하루 마무리

 MP3 **114**

갠 빨래를 서랍장에 넣다
put the folded laundry in
the drawer

손톱/발톱을 다듬다
trim one's nails /
toenails

안마의자/안마기로 마사지하다
massage with a massage
chair / a massager

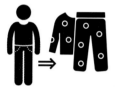

잠옷으로 갈아입다
change into
one's pajamas

애인/친구/가족에게
전화하다
call one's lover /
friend / family

내일 일정을 확인하다
check tomorrow's
schedule

누워서 스마트폰으로
인터넷을 하다
lie down and use the
Internet on one's smartphone

알람을 맞추다
set an alarm

핸드폰을 충전기에 꽂다
plug one's cell phone
into a charger

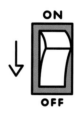

방의 전등을 끄다
turn off the light
in one's room

잠자리에 들다
go to bed

SENTENCES TO USE

퇴근 후에 집에서 안마의자로 마사지하는 거야말로 완벽한 하루 마무리이죠.
Massaging with a massage chair at home after work is the perfect end of the day.

잠옷으로 갈아입고 친구에게 전화할 거예요.
I am going to call my friend after I change into my pajamas.

저는 누워서 스마트폰으로 내일 일정을 확인하는 습관이 있습니다.
I have a habit of lying down and checking tomorrow's schedule on my smartphone.

그는 알람을 맞춰 놓지 않아서 시험에 늦었습니다.
He was late for an exam because he didn't set his alarm clock.

잠자리에 들기 전에 충전기에 휴대폰 꽂는 것 잊지 마세요!
Don't forget to plug your cell phone into a charger before you go to bed!

15

주말 & 휴일

WEEKEND & HOLIDAYS

아이스박스에 음식을 챙기다
pack food
in an ice box

캠핑 장비를 챙기다
pack one's camping
equipment

텐트를/그늘막을 치다
set up a tent /
a shade

텐트를/그늘막을 치우다
clear a tent /
a shade

그늘에 돗자리를 깔다
spread [lay] a mat
in the shade

시냇가에서 물장구치다
play in the water
by the stream

휴대용 랜턴을 켜다
turn on a portable
lantern

반조리(인스턴트) 식품을 데우다
heat up precooked
foods [meals]

숯에 불을 지피다
set charcoal on fire,
fire up the charcoal

숯불에 고기를 굽다
barbecue [grill meat]
on charcoal

모닥불 주위에 둘러앉다
sit around a
campfire [a bonfire]

야영지를 정리하다
clean up one's
campsite

SENTENCES TO USE

텐트 치는 걸 보면 그 사람이 (캠핑) 초보자라는 걸 알 수 있습니다.
You can tell that he is a newbie by looking at the way he sets up a tent.

그늘에 돗자리 깔고 아이들 물놀이를 하게 하는 건 어떨까요?
Why don't we lay the mat in the shade and let the kids play in the water?

랜턴 켜고 숯불 좀 피워 줄래요?
Can you turn on the lantern and fire up the charcoal?

얼른 와요! 모닥불에 둘러앉아 마시멜로를 굽자고요.
Come on! Let's sit around the bonfire and roast some marshmallows.

저는 사람들이 텐트 걷고 나서 야영지를 정리하지 않는 게 싫어요.
I hate it when people don't clean up their campsite after clearing the tent.

간단한 음식과 음료를 챙기다
pack simple food
and drinks

도시 외곽에서 바람 쐬다
get some fresh air outside
[at the outskirts of] the city

경치 좋은 곳에서 드라이브를 하다
take a drive
in a scenic spot

경관을 둘러보다
look around the
landscape

신선한 공기를 들이마시다
breathe in fresh air

박물관/전시관/수목원의 표를 끊다
get a ticket to a museum / an
exhibition hall / an arboretum

안내 책자를 받다
get a brochure

안내원의 설명을 듣다
listen to the guide's
explanation

~와 스냅사진을 찍다
take a snapshot
with ~

셀카를 찍다
take a selfie

SENTENCES TO USE

저는 주말마다 도시 외곽에서 바람 쐬려고 차를 구입했습니다.
I bought a car to get some fresh air outside the city every weekend.

남자 친구와 저는 교외의 경치 좋은 곳에서 드라이브를 했습니다.
My boyfriend and I took a drive in a scenic spot on the outskirts.

가끔은 신선한 공기를 들이마시는 게 중요하죠.
It is important to breathe in fresh air once in a while.

명절에는 전시회 티켓을 구하기가 어렵습니다.
It is hard to get tickets to an exhibition during holidays.

아무도 제 사진을 찍어 주지 않기 때문에 전 보통 셀카를 찍습니다.
I usually take a selfie because no one takes a photo for me.

A 오늘 야구 경기 너무 재밌었어,
그렇지?
▶ That was a great baseball
game today, right?

B 완전! 9회 2아웃 상황에서 타자가
끝내기 역전 홈런을 때릴지 누가
상상이나 했겠어?
● Totally! Who would have
imagined that the batter
would hit a grand slam to win
a losing game with two outs in
the ninth inning?

우리 팀이 5대 2로 질 줄 알았는데
갑자기 6대 5로 이기고 끝나니
흥분이 가시지 않네.
● I thought our team would
lose 5 to 2, but I am still so
hyped after winning 6 to 5.

A 그러게 말이야.
▶ I know.

상대 팀 응원석 보니까 다들 어이가
없어서 넋이 나갔던데.
▶ When I looked at the
opponent's cheering section,
everyone was speechless and
lost their minds.

B 엄청 허무했을 거야. 다 이긴 줄
알았을 테니까.
● They must have been
dumbstruck, since they
thought they won.

A 게임도 끝났는데 이제 뭐 할까?
▶ What should we do now
that the game is over?

B 뭐 좀 먹자. 이 근처에 맛집 뭐 있나
인터넷으로 찾아볼래?
● Let's eat something. Can
you look for a good place
around here on the Internet?

A 음. 여기서 300미터 떨어진
지하철역 근처에 유명한
돈가스집이 있어.
▶ Hmm. There is a famous
pork cutlet restaurant near the
subway station 300 meters
away from here.

TV에도 여러 번 나왔던
음식점인데 리뷰가 엄청 좋아.
가격도 저렴한 편이고.
▶ It was on TV several times
and the reviews are really
good. It's inexpensive, too.

B   그래? 잘됐네. 거기서 돈가스 먹고
    제임스강 공원으로 산책하러 가자.
    ● Really? That's good. Let's eat
    pork cutlets there and go for a
    walk in James River Park.

A   검색해 보니까 제임스강 공원
    입구에서 남쪽으로 2킬로미터쯤
    가면 제임스강 유람선 탈 수 있는
    곳이 있어.
    ▶ I looked it up and there is a
    place where we can take the
    James River cruise 2 kilometers
    south of the James River Park
    entrance.

    그거 해보는 거 어때?
    ▶ Why don't we try that?

B   아주 좋은 생각이야. 2 킬로미터면
    거리가 좀 머니까 자전거 타자.
    ● That's a great idea. It's a
    little far if it is 2 kilometers, so
    let's take a bike.

A   좋아. 유람선 타고 강 건너편에서
    내리면 그쪽에 전망 좋은 카페가
    있어.
    ▶ Sure. If we take the cruise
    ship and get off the other side
    of the river, there is a cafe with
    a good view.

    거기서 커피 마시면서 일몰 보자.
    ▶ Let's drink coffee there and
    enjoy the sunset.

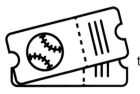

경기 티켓을 끊다
get [buy] a
ticket to a game

응원 도구를 챙기다
pack one's cheering gear

경기장에 가다
go to the stadium [game]

응원단과 구호를 외치다
chant with the cheering squad

치어리더의 공연을 보다
watch a cheerleader
performance

전광판에서 경기/선수 정보를 확인하다
check the game / player information
on the electronic display

SENTENCES TO USE

응원 도구 챙기는 걸 잊었다면 파도타기를 하면서 응원해야 할 것 같아.
If you forgot to pack your cheering gear, we are going to have to cheer by doing
the waves.

치어리더 공연을 볼 때는 존중하는 자세를 보여주세요.
Please show some respect when you are watching a cheerleader performance.

새로 들어온 선수가 있어서 전광판에서 선수 정보를 확인해야 합니다.
We need to check the player information on the electronic display because there is
a new player.

상대팀에게 야유를 보내다
boo [jeer] one's opposing team

선수의 실수/부상에 안타까워하다
be sorry for the player's mistake / injury

득점에 박수를 치다
applaud for scoring

파도타기 응원을 하다
cheer by doing the waves

승리한 선수들을 응원하다
cheer for the victorious players

패배한 선수들을 격려하다
cheer up the defeated players

야유를 퍼붓고 상대 팀을 방해하는 것은 스포츠맨답지 않습니다.
Booing and interrupting the opposing team is not very sportsmanlike.

패배한 팀을 놀리지 말고 격려하는 것이 중요합니다.
It is important to cheer up the defeated team instead of teasing them.

인터넷으로 맛집을 검색하다
search for must-eat [good]
restaurants on the Internet

외식 장소를 예약하다
reserve a place to eat

대기 명단에 이름을 올리다
put one's name on the waiting list

메뉴를 고르다
choose a menu [a dish]

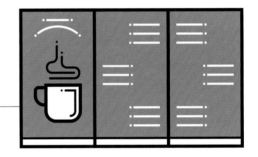

식사를 주문하다
order a meal

종업원에게 인기 메뉴를 물어보다
ask the server about the popular menu

SENTENCES TO USE

에이 참! 깜빡하고 자리를 예약하지 않아서 대기자 명단에 이름을 올려야 해요.
Darn it! I forgot to reserve a table, so we have to put our name on the waiting list.

무엇을 주문할지 결정할 수 없다면, 종업원에게 인기 메뉴를 물어보는 건 어때요?
If you can't decide what to order, why not ask the server about the popular menu?

음식을 추가로 주문하다
order more [extra] food

숟가락을/포크를/젓가락을 달라고 하다
ask for a spoon / a fork / chopsticks

가족/친구와 식사를 즐기다
enjoy a meal with one's family / friend

계산서를 요청하다
ask for the bill

남은 음식을 포장하다
pack the leftovers

음식 맛에 항의하다
complain about the taste of food

누나가 인터넷에서 이 식당을 찾았고, 우리는 식사 내내 즐거웠습니다.
My sister found this restaurant on the Internet, and we enjoyed the whole meal.

우리는 계산서를 요청하고 각자 나눠서 계산했습니다.
We asked for the bill and split the check.

집에 있는 우리 개 갖다주게 남은 음식을 포장해 가려고 해요.
I am going to pack my leftover for my dog at home.

에어컨/난방을 세게 틀어 놓다
crank up the air
conditioner / heating

실내에서 날씨를 즐기다
enjoy the weather
from indoors

밀키트로 요리를 하다
cook with meal kits

~로 간단히 요기하다
(대충 때우다)
make do with ~

즉석밥을 전자레인지에 돌리다
microwave instant
[pre-cooked] rice

멍 때리다
space [zone] out

가족과 대화를 나누다
have a conversation
with one's family

취미 생활을 하다
have [pursue]
a hobby

밀린 빨래를 하다
do one's (piled-up) laundry
behind schedule

밀린 TV 드라마를 몰아보다
catch up on [binge-
watch] TV dramas

책을 읽다
read
a book

SENTENCES TO USE

저는 에어컨을 세게 켜고 푹신한 이불 속으로 들어가는 걸 좋아합니다.
I love to crank up the AC and get under my fluffy blanket.

1인 가구들이 밀키트로 요리하는 것이 현재 추세입니다.
It is a current trend for one-person households to cook with meal kits.

그냥 점심때 남은 음식으로 대충 때우죠.
Let's just make do with leftovers from last lunch.

저는 침대에 멍 때리고 있는 것 외에는 아무것도 하기 싫어요.
I don't like to do anything but space out on my bed.

테레사는 밀린 드라마를 몰아 봐야 해서 주말에 우리를 만나지 않을 거예요.
Theresa is not meeting us on the weekend because she needs to binge-watch her dramas.

(종교)를 믿다
believe in

교회/성당/절에 가다
go to church / Catholic church /
Buddhist temple

~로 개종하다
convert to ~

(아직) 종교가 없다
have no religion (yet)

무신론자가 되다
be an atheist

타 종교를 배척하다
exclude [reject] other religions

타 종교를 포용하다
embrace [tolerate]
other religions

성지 순례를 가다
go on a
pilgrimage

사이비 종교에 빠지다
get into [fall for] a pseudo-
religion [a cult]

SENTENCES TO USE

어머니는 천주교 신자였지만 10년 전에 불교로 개종하셨습니다.
My mother was a Catholic but she converted to Buddhism 10 years ago.

종교가 없다고 해서 제가 무신론자인 것은 아닙니다.
Not having a religion does not mean that I am an atheist.

몇몇 종교는 신도들에게 성지 순례를 가라고 요구합니다.
Several religions require believers to go on a pilgrimage.

그의 가족 모두가 사이비 종교에 빠져 어느 날 사라졌다는 소식 들었어요?
Did you hear that his whole family got into a cult and vanished one day?

예배에 참석하다
attend a
service

교회에 다니다
attend church

5:30 AM

새벽 예배에 가다
attend an early
morning service

2:00 AM

철야 예배를 드리다
hold an all-night service

온라인으로 예배를 드리다
attend an online
worship service

찬송가를 부르다
sing a hymn
[songs of praise]

헌금하다
give [make]
an offering

설교를 듣다
listen to
the sermon

십일조를 내다
give tithes,
tithe

전도하다
evangelize

성경을 읽다/필사하다
read / transcribe
the Bible

성경 공부를 하다/
성경 공부 모임에 참석하다
study the Bible / participate
in a Bible study group

Christianity

교리 교육을 받다
take a
baptism class

SENTENCES TO USE

제 조부모님은 매주 월요일에 새벽 예배에 가시곤 하셨습니다.
My grandparents used to attend an early morning service every Monday.

부득이한 사정으로 인해 이번 주는 온라인 예배가 진행됩니다.
Due to unavoidable circumstances, worship service will be held online this week.

제 남동생은 교회에서 찬송가를 부르는 성가대 소년이었어요.
My brother was a choirboy singing hymns at church.

그는 설교를 듣다가 잠이 들었습니다.
He fell asleep while listening to the sermon.

저는 유학 시절 성경 공부 모임에 참석했습니다.
I participated in a Bible study group when I was studying abroad.

교회 수련회에 가다
go to a church retreat

부흥회에 참석하다
attend a revival
(meeting)

기도원에 가서 기도하다
go to the house of
prayer to pray

간증하다
give a
testimony

부활절 앞두고 40일 금식을 하다
fast for 40 days
ahead of Easter

주일학교 선생님을 하다
teach Sunday school, become
a Sunday school teacher

집사/장로에 임명되다
be appointed deacon
[deaconess] / elder

목사님 축도를 받다
get blessed by
a pastor

주기도문/사도신경을 암송하다
recite the Lord's Prayer /
Apostles' Creed

교회 주보를 읽다
read a weekly
church news [report]

교회 성가대에 서다
stand in one's
church choir

SENTENCES TO USE

저는 예전에 교회 수련회에 가는 것을 좋아했습니다.
I used to like going to a church retreat.

어머니는 기도하러 기도원에 몇 주씩 가시곤 해서 저와 제 남매는 그것이 전혀 마음에 들지 않았습니다.
My mother used to go to the house of prayer to pray for weeks at a time, so my siblings and I didn't like it at all.

다니엘은 항상 청년부 주일학교 선생님이 되고 싶었습니다.
Daniel always wanted to become a Sunday school teacher for the youth.

고모가 우리 교회의 새 집사(권사)로 임명되었습니다.
My aunt was appointed as the new deaconess of our church.

데브라는 교회 성가대에 서서 마음껏 노래를 불렀습니다.
Debra stood in her church choir and sang her heart out.

미사를 드리다
go to mass

부활절/크리스마스 미사를 드리다
give an Easter / a Christmas Mass

온라인으로 미사를 드리다
attend mass online

묵주 기도를 드리다
pray the rosary

강론을 듣다
listen to the sermon

성호를 긋다
cross oneself

미사포를 쓰다
wear a veil

(유아) 세례를 받다
be baptized
(as a baby)

세례명을 받다
be christened ~ /
get a baptismal name

고해성사를 하다
go to [make a] confession,
confess (one's sins)

영성체를 하다
take [receive]
communion

SENTENCES TO USE

그는 손에 묵주를 들고 강론을 들었습니다.
He listened to the sermon with a rosary in his hands.

그녀는 기도할 때 성호를 그었습니다.
She crossed herself when she was praying.

여성들은 기도할 때 미사포를 쓰는 것이 관례입니다.
It is customary for women to wear veils when they pray.

셀레나는 유아 세례를 받았습니다.
Selena was baptized as a baby.

고해성사를 얼마나 자주 해야 할까요?
How often do you have to go to confession?

피정을 가다
go on a (religious) retreat

냉담자가 되다
become a lapsed Catholic

기도 모임을 갖다
hold a prayer
meeting

대모/대부가 되다
become one's godmother /
godfather

기도문을 암송하다
recite a prayer

교적을 옮기다
move from church to church

SENTENCES TO USE

루나는 아버지가 돌아가신 후 냉담자가 되었습니다.
Luna became a lapsed Catholic after her father passed away.

가장 친한 친구가 내게 자기 딸의 대부가 되어 달라고 부탁했습니다.
My best friend asked me to become her daughter's godfather.

예불을 드리다
attend a
Buddhist service

불공을 드리다
pray to Buddha,
offer a Buddhist prayer,
worship in the Buddhist temple

합장하다
put one's hands together
in front of the chest
[as if in prayer]

염주를 돌리며 기도하다
count one's beads

불경을 (소리 내어) 읽다
read the Buddhist
scriptures (out loud)

절을 하다
make a deep bow

108배를 하다
make one hundred
and eight bows

향을 피우다
burn incense

연등을 달다
hang [put] up a lotus lantern

연등/촛불을 밝히다
light a lotus lantern / a candle

SENTENCES TO USE

매년 부처님 오신 날에 수천 명이 함께하는 불교 예불이 있습니다.
There is an annual Buddhist service with thousands of people on the Day of Buddha's Coming.

스님들은 큰 소리로 불경을 읽습니다. The monks read the Buddhist scriptures out loud.

매일 108배 하느라 제 무릎 연골이 닳았어요.
I've worn out my knee cartilage by making 108 bows every day.

저는 절의 목탁 소리와 향 피우는 냄새가 좋습니다.
I like the sound of moktak and the smell of burning incense at the temple.

어머니는 우리 가족 모두를 위해 연등을 밝히셨습니다.
My mother lit a lotus lantern for our whole family.

출가하다
become a
Buddhist monk

목탁을 두드리다
beat [tap, knock on] a moktak
(Buddhist wooden gong)

수행하다
practice
asceticism

참선하다
do Zen meditation,
do zazen

템플 스테이에 참가하다
participate in [join]
temple stay

탑을 돌다(탑돌이를 하다)
circle the pagoda

법명을 받다
get [receive] one's
Buddhist name

윤회 사상을 이해하다
understand the concept of
reincarnation [rebirth]

설법을 듣다
listen to the monk's
sermon

시주하다
give alms, donate [offer]
money / rice

SENTENCES TO USE

그는 어린 나이에 출가했습니다.
He became a Buddhist monk at an early age.

많은 외국인들이 템플 스테이에 참가하는 것을 좋아합니다.
A lot of foreigners like to participate in temple stay.

그녀는 스님으로부터 법명을 받게 되어 영광이었습니다.
She was honored to get her Buddhist name from the monk.

신자들이 윤회의 개념을 이해하는 건 쉽지 않습니다.
It is not easy for believers to understand the concept of reincarnation.

불교 신자은 항상 쌀과 과일 같은 시주를 바칩니다.
Buddhist devotees always give alms such as rice and fruits.

여행

TRAVEL

여행 준비

여행 계획을 세우다
plan a trip, make [come up with] a travel plan

여행 예산을 짜다
figure out one's travel budget

여행지를 정하다
choose [decide on]
a place [a location] to travel,
decide on one's travel destination

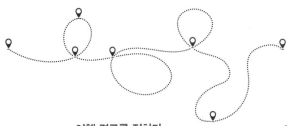

여행 경로를 정하다
set a course for one's trip

여권 만료일을 확인하다
check the expiration date of
one's passport

SENTENCES TO USE

여행지를 정하기 전에 여행 예산부터 짜는 것이 현명해 보입니다.
It seems wise to figure out your travel budget before you decide on a location to travel.

당신이 여권 만료일을 확인하지 않았다니 믿기지 않아요!
I can't believe you didn't check the expiration date of your passport!

여권용/비자용 사진을 찍다
take a passport / visa picture

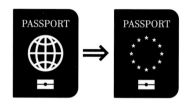

여권을 재발급받다
get one's passport reissued

비자를 발급받다
get a visa

국제 운전면허를 발급받다
get one's international driver's license issued

여행자 보험에 가입하다
take out travel insurance

필수 예방 접종을 받다
get mandatory vaccinations

온라인으로 쉽게 신청해서 비자를 받을 수 있습니다.
You can easily apply online and get a visa.

해외에서 차를 렌트할 계획이라면 국제 운전면허 발급받는 거 잊지 마세요.
Don't forget to get your international driver's license issued if you are planning on renting a car overseas.

다행히도, 수는 여행자 보험에 들었고 여행 중에 고장 난 핸드폰 보상을 받았습니다.
Fortunately, Sue took out travel insurance and got compensation for her broken cellphone during her travel.

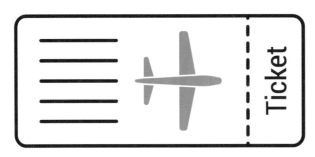

~ 행 비행기표/기차표를
예약하다
book a flight /
train ticket to ~

호텔을/리조트를/호스텔을/민박을 예약하다
book [reserve] a hotel / a resort /
a hostel / a B&B

티켓/서류 사본을 만들어 놓다
make copies of tickets / documents

현지 날씨를 확인하다
check the local weather

여행 짐을 싸다(꾸리다)
pack up one's travel luggage

SENTENCES TO USE

케이트는 마드리드행 비행기표를 예약하고 싶었지만 남은 표가 없었습니다.
Kate wanted to book a flight ticket to Madrid, but there were no seats left.

인터넷으로 현지 날씨 확인하고 그에 맞게 옷을 싸세요.
Check the local weather on the Internet and pack clothes accordingly.

구급약/처방약/비타민을 챙기다
pack first-aid medicine / prescription
medicine [drugs] / vitamins

여행용 어댑터를 챙기다
pack a travel adapter

여행 용품과 화장품 샘플들을 싸다
pack up travel supplies and
cosmetics samples

신용카드를 발급받다
get a credit card issued

수수료가 낮을 때 환전하다
exchange money when the
commission is low

모든 예약을 다시 확인하다
confirm [recheck] all
reservations

해외에서 휴대폰 충전하고 싶다면 잊지 말고 여행용 어댑터 챙기세요!
Don't forget to pack a travel adapter if you want to charge your phone overseas!

앰버는 여행에 쓸 화장품 샘플을 많이 모았습니다.
Amber saved a lot of cosmetics samples for her travels.

해외 결제 수수료가 가장 저렴해서 이 신용카드를 발급받았습니다.
I got this credit card issued because its foreign transaction fee is the lowest.

저는 공항으로 출발하기 전에 모든 예약을 다시 확인하는 습관이 있습니다.
I have a habit of rechecking all reservations before I leave for the airport.

A 자기야, 이번 휴가 때 어디로 갈지 생각해 봤어?

▶ Darling, have you given any thoughts about where to go for this vacation?

B 응, 발리는 많이 가 봤으니까 이번에는 다른 곳에 가 보는 게 어때?

● Yes, since we've been to Bali a lot, how about we go to other places this time?

A 음, 그런데 자기 올해 여권 만기 되는 것 같던데 여권 날짜는 괜찮아?

▶ Hmm, I thought your passport expires this year. Is the expiration date okay?

B 괜찮아. 아직 만기까지 8개월 남았어. 해외여행 가는 데 문제없을 거야.

● It's fine. I still have 8 more months until expiration. There should be no problem traveling overseas.

A 태국 패키지 여행은 어때? 아니면 자유 여행으로 갈까?

▶ How about a package tour to Thailand? Or a self-planned trip?

B 태국은 패키지로 몇 번 가 봤으니까 이번에는 자유 여행으로 괌 어때?

● We have been on a package tour to Thailand a few times, so how about a self-planned trip to Guam?

A 좋아. 그런데 할인이 많아서 패키지 여행이 항공권이랑 호텔을 따로 예약해야 하는 자유 여행보다 더 쌀 수도 있어.

▶ Okay, but due to lots of discounts, package tours can be cheaper than self-planned trips where we need to book flights and hotels separately.

요즘은 패키지 여행에도 옵션 좋고 자유 시간 주는 것이 있어.

▶ There are good options and free times for package tours nowadays.

B 하지만 패키지 여행 가면 의무적으로 쇼핑몰에서 쇼핑하고 그래야 하는 거 아냐?

● But don't package tours have mandatory shopping time at the malls and stuff?

A 그렇기는 한데, 얼른 둘러보고
맛난 거 사 먹고 쇼핑몰 안에 있는
곳에서 마사지 받으면 될 것 같은데.
▶ That's true, but I think we
can just have a quick look, eat
something and get a massage
inside the shopping mall or
something.

B 휴가까지 얼마 안 남았는데
이것저것 알아보는 것도
불편할 것 같아.
● There is not much time left
until vacation, and it seems
inconvenient to look into this
and that.

패키지 여행 상품으로 알아보자.
● Let's go with the package
tour.

호텔은 조식 풀 패키지 옵션으로
선택하는 게 편하겠어.
● It would be better to
choose the hotel with the full
breakfast package option.

A 좋았어! 그동안 모아 놓은 면세점
할인 쿠폰 많은데 이번에 괌 갈 때
면세점 들러서 필요한 것들 살 때
써야겠어.
▶ Awesome! I have a lot of
duty-free discount coupons
saved up which I will use at the
duty-free shops on our way
to Guam and buy things that I
need.

B 나도! 나도 향수 거의 다 떨어져
가는데, 면세점에서 사야겠다.
● Me, too! I am out of
perfume, so I should buy it at
the duty-free.

그러면 자기가 괌 여행 패키지
상품 좀 알아봐 줄 수 있어?
● Then can you look for the
package tour for Guam?

여행자 보험은 가기 전에 같이
가입하면 될 것 같아.
● I think we can take out
travel insurance together
before we go.

공항 체크인 카운터에서 체크인하다
check in at the airport check-in counter

보안 검색을 받다/통과하다
get / pass through a security check

비행기를 타다
board [get on] a plane

연결 항공편을 기다리다
wait for one's connecting flight

출입국 심사를 받다
go through immigration

출입국 심사관의 질문에 대답하다
answer the immigration officer's questions

SENTENCES TO USE

전 공항 체크인 카운터에서 체크인하고 짐을 부치는 느낌이 너무 좋아요.
I love the feeling of checking in at the airport check-in counter and sending my baggage.

우리는 연결 항공편을 4시간 넘게 기다렸습니다.
We waited over 4 hours for our connecting flight.

제가 질문에 대답을 잘못해서 출입국 관리 직원이 몇 시간 동안 질문을 했나 봐요!
I guess the immigration officer questioned me for hours because I answered his questions wrong!

여권에 도장을 받다
get one's passport stamped

세관을 통과하다
go [pass] through customs

세관에 걸리다
be caught in customs

수하물 찾는 곳에서 짐을 찾다
pick up one's luggage at the
baggage claim

숙소 행 셔틀을 타다
take a shuttle to one's
accommodation

유진은 면세 한도를 초과해서 세관에 걸렸습니다.
Eugene was caught in customs because he went over his duty-free limit.

수하물 찾는 곳에서 짐 찾은 후 셔틀을 타고 숙소로 가시면 됩니다.
You can take a shuttle to your accommodation after picking up your luggage at the
baggage claim.

면세점 & 현지 쇼핑

기념품을 사다
purchase [buy] souvenirs

면세점을 구경하다
look around duty-free shops

공항 면세점에서 ~를 구입하다
purchase [buy] ~ at the duty-free shop at the airport

면세 주류를 구매하다
purchase [buy] duty-free liquor

명품을 저렴한 값에 구매하다
purchase [buy] luxury goods at a low price

SENTENCES TO USE

면세점을 둘러본 지 정말 오래되었네요!
It has been a while since I looked around duty-free shops!

그녀의 남자 친구는 면세 주류 몇 병을 샀습니다.
Her boyfriend purchased a few bottles of duty-free liquor.

이 명품 지갑을 저렴한 가격에 살 수 있어서 전 운이 좋았습니다.
I was lucky to be able to buy this luxury brand wallet at a low price.

면세점 할인 쿠폰을 사용하다
use duty-free discount coupons

면세 한도액을 확인하다
check the duty-free limit

온라인에서 구매한 면세품을 픽업하다
pick up duty-free goods purchased online

현지에서만 구매 가능한 물건을 사다
buy goods that can only be
purchased locally

(~에게) 부탁받은 물건을 구매하다
purchase [buy] a requested item,
buy something that ~ asked for

온라인에서 구매한 면세점 화장품을 찾는 건 신이 납니다.
It's exciting to pick up duty-free cosmetics I purchased online.
저는 백화점에서 언니가 부탁한 페이스 크림을 샀습니다.
I bought a face cream that my sister asked for at the department store.

~에서 체크아웃하다
check out of ~

~에 체크인하다
check into ~

호텔 직원에게 여행 정보를 문의하다
ask the hotel staff for travel information

호텔의 무료 서비스를 이용하다
take advantage of hotel
complimentary services

호텔과 연계된 관광지 할인을 받다
get a discount on tourist attractions
affiliated to one's hotel

룸서비스를 시키다
order room service

SENTENCES TO USE

호텔 직원에게 여행 정보를 물었더니 관광지 할인에 대해 말해 줬습니다.
When I asked the hotel staff for travel information, he told me about a discount on tourist attractions.

제 조카는 부모님 허락 없이 룸서비스를 시켜서 혼났습니다.
My niece got into trouble for ordering room service without her parent's permission.

MP3 130

조식 뷔페를 먹다
have [eat] a breakfast buffet

호텔 수영장을 이용하다
use the hotel swimming pool

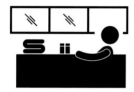

~와 호캉스를 즐기다
enjoy a hotel vacation [staycation] with ~

스파에서 마사지를 받다
get a massage at a spa

오션 뷰/마운틴 뷰를 만끽하다
enjoy the sea / mountain view

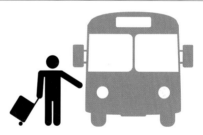

셔틀 서비스를 이용하다
use a shuttle service

우리가 호텔 수영장에 있을 때 비가 내리기 시작했습니다.
It started to rain when we were at the hotel swimming pool.

저는 지난 주말에 친구들과 호캉스를 즐겼습니다.
I enjoyed a hotel staycation with my friends last weekend.

그녀는 스파에서 마사지를 받으면서 오션 뷰 즐기는 것을 좋아합니다.
She likes to enjoy the sea view while getting a massage at the spa.

(~로) 여행 가다
go on a trip to ~, travel to ~

one-day trip

~로 당일치기 여행을 가다
go on a one-day trip to ~

배낭여행을 가다
go backpacking,
go on a backpacking trip

가이드 투어에 참여하다
take part in a
guided tour

패키지 여행을 가다
go on a package tour

국내 여행을 하다
make [go on] a
domestic trip

SENTENCES TO USE

이번 여름에 가족들과 런던으로 여행 갈 계획입니다.
I'm planning to go on a trip to London with my family this summer.

패키지 여행보다는 배낭여행을 가는 게 더 낫겠어요.
I'd rather go on a backpacking trip than go on a package tour.

해외여행을 하다
travel abroad

세계 일주를 하다
travel around the world

도보로 국토 종단 여행을 하다
go on a cross-country walking trip

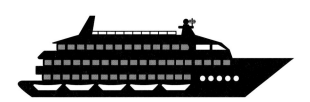

크루즈 여행을 하다/~를 크루즈 여행을 보내주다
go on a cruise / send ~ on a cruise

야시장에 가 보다
go to the night market

대부분의 사람들은 은퇴 후 세계 여행을 하는 꿈이 있습니다.
Most people have a dream of traveling around the world after they retire.

저는 20대 초반에 국토 종단 도보 여행을 했는데 제가 한 최고의 경험이었습니다.
I went on a cross-country walking trip in my early 20s and it was the best experience I had.

조부모님이 제 졸업 선물로 크루즈 여행을 보내 주셨어요.
My grandparents sent me on a cruise for my graduation gift.

야시장 보러 가요! 재미있다고 들었어요.
Let's go visit the night market! I heard it's fun.

MP3 132

관광 명소에 가다
visit [go to] a tourist
attraction

관광을 즐기다
enjoy
sightseeing

~의 사진을 찍다
take a photo of ~,
photograph ~

현지 맛집들을 찾아가다
visit [go to] local
restaurants

현지 음식을 먹어 보다
try local food

현지 문화를 체험하다
experience the
local culture

~의 야경을 감상하다
enjoy the night
view of ~

SENTENCES TO USE

유명한 관광지 사진을 찍는 것은 신납니다.
It's exciting to take a photo of famous tourist attractions.

저는 여행할 때 항상 이색적이고 희귀한 현지 음식을 먹어 봅니다.
I always try local exotic and rare food when I travel.

그들은 도시 야경을 즐기기 위해 고층 빌딩에 올라갔습니다.
They went up the skyscraper to enjoy the night view of the city.

여행을 마치고 돌아오다
come back from one's trip

SNS에 여행 사진과 후기를 올리다
post pictures and reviews of
the trip on SNS

여행 사진 앨범을 만들다
make a travel
photo album

~에게 여행 경험을 이야기하다
talk to ~ about one's
travel experience

저는 여행할 때 SNS에 사진 올리는 것을 절대 잊지 않습니다.
I never forget to post pictures on SNS when I am traveling.

그는 여행에서 돌아오자마자 친구들에게 자기 여행 경험을 이야기했습니다.
He told his friends about his travel experience as soon as he came back from his trip.

주(state)마다 가격이 다른 판매세

미국에 여행 와서 물건을 사거나 음식점에서 식사한 후에 결제할 때 예상보다 비용이 훨씬 많이 나와서 당황할 때가 많습니다. 왜 가격표에 붙은 가격보다 더 많은 돈을 내야 하는지 지금부터 알아볼까요?

미국의 판매세(Sales Taxes)는 우리나라의 부가가치세(Value Added Tax: VAT)와 비슷한 개념이지만 납부 방식은 매우 다릅니다. 먼저 미국의 판매세는 징수하는 주체가 연방정부(Federal Government)가 아닌 주정부(State Government)입니다. 두 번째로 우리나라에서는 판매 제품에 10%의 부가가치세를 반영하여 상품의 최종 가격이 정해지지만, 미국은 주에 따라 다른 세율로 판매세가 산정되며, 제품에 표시된 가격은 판매세가 붙지 않은 면세 가격입니다. 그래서 미국에서는 물건을 계산할 때 주마다 정해져 있는 세율에 맞춰 판매세를 추가로 내야 하는 것이죠. 판매세는 Sales Tax와 Local Tax라는 두 가지 세금의 합산으로 산정되는데, Sales Tax는 주 정부에서 부과하는 소비세고, Local Tax는 지방 정부 소비세입니다.

미국 주마다 판매세 범위는 매우 다양합니다. 델라웨어(DE), 오리건(OR), 뉴햄프셔(NH)주의 경우는 판매세 자체를 전혀 부과하지 않아 상품에 붙어 있는 가격대로 결제가 되

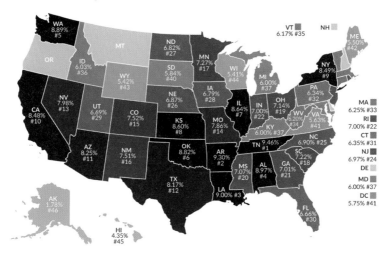

How High Are Sales Taxes in Your State?

Combined State & Average Local Sales Tax Rates, 2016

VT 6.17% #35   NH

WA 8.89% #5

MT

OR

ID 6.03% #36

ND 6.82% #27

MN 7.27% #17

WI 5.41% #44

MI 6.00% #37

NY 8.49% #9

ME 5.50% #42

WY 5.42% #43

SD 5.84% #40

IA 6.79% #28

PA 6.34% #32

NV 7.98% #13

UT 6.69% #29

CO 7.52% #15

NE 6.87% #26

IL 8.64% #7

IN 7.00% #22

OH 7.14% #19

WV 6.20% #34

VA 5.63% #41

MA 6.25% #33

CA 8.48% #10

KS 8.60% #8

MO 7.86% #14

KY 6.00% #37

RI 7.00% #22

CT 6.35% #31

AZ 8.25% #11

NM 7.51% #16

OK 8.82% #6

AR 9.30% #2

TN 9.46% #1

NC 6.90% #25

SC 7.22% #18

NJ 6.97% #24

DE

TX 8.17% #12

MS 7.07% #20

AL 8.97% #4

GA 7.01% #21

MD 6.00% #37

LA 9.00% #3

DC 5.75% #41

AK 1.78% #46

FL 6.66% #30

HI 4.35% #45

Note: City, county, and municipal rates vary. These rates are weighted by population to compute an average local tax rate. Three states levy mandatory, statewide local add-on sales taxes at the state level: California (1%), Utah (1.25%), and Virginia (1%). We include these in their state sales tax rates. The sales taxes in Hawaii, New Mexico, and South Dakota have broad bases that include many business-to-business services. Due to data limitations, the table does not include sales taxes in local resort areas in Montana. Some counties in New Jersey are not subject to statewide sales tax rates and collect a local rate of 3.5%. Their average local score is represented as a negative.
Source: Sales Tax Clearinghouse; Tax Foundation calculations.

Combined Sales Tax Rate

Lower   Higher

TAX FOUNDATION   @TaxFoundation

어 상대적으로 저렴하게 상품을 구입할 수 있습니다. 그래서 우리나라 사람들이 미국 직구를 할 때 판매세가 없어 더 저렴한 델라웨어, 오리건, 뉴햄프셔주 판매점에서 구입하는 것을 선호하는 것이죠.

하지만 루이지애나(LA), 테네시(TN), 아칸소(AR), 워싱턴(WA)주의 경우, 상품 가격에 9% 이상의 판매세를 내야 해서 상대적으로 소비자에게 큰 부담이 되기도 합니다. 미국에서 물건을 살 때, 특히나 온라인 쇼핑을 할 때는 판매자 주소지에 따라 판매세가 다르게 부과되니 판매세가 저렴한 주에 주소지를 둔 판매처에서 구입을 해야 비용을 아낄 수 있습니다.

INDEX 색인 찾아보기

한글 인덱스

ㅂ

ㅋ

ㅌ

기타

INDEX 색인 찾아보기

영어 인덱스

F

329

K

L

339

R

V

W

Z